# ACE YOUR JOB SEARCH

## The Interactive Workbook for Career Success

Gain Clarity, Build Confidence & Achieve the Career You Deserve

## THE PROVEN FORMULA

I + Plan + Marketing + Action = Success™

# SUJAYKUMAR VARDHMANE
Leadership & Human Capital Strategist

**STRATEGIC HUMAN CAPITAL INC**

**Book Title:** *ACE Your Job Search*
**Author:** Sujaykumar Vardhmane

(E-book) ISBN: 978-1-7752873-2-2
(Paperback) ISBN: 978-1-7752873-0-8
(Hardcover) ISBN: 978-1-7752873-1-5

Printed in Canada
**Book Cover & Book Design by:** Strategic Human Capital, Inc.

This is a work of ideas, products, and concepts of the author's imagination. Any resemblance to an actual person's ideas, products, and concepts are entirely coincidental.
No part of this book may be reproduced or stored in a retrieval system, or transmitted in any form or by any means, electronic, mechanical, photocopying, recording, or otherwise, without written permission from the author.

*Ace Your Job Search* is your practical, step-by-step companion to better understand every stage of the job hunt with confidence and clarity. Whether you're a recent graduate, a mid-career professional seeking a change, someone re-entering the workforce, or looking to guide your mentee, this book offers real-world insights and proven strategies to help you stand out and succeed.

Grounded in over three decades of Human Resources and leadership experience, the author presents a holistic framework, I + Plan + Marketing + Action = Success, that integrates self-assessment, career planning, résumé and LinkedIn optimization, networking, and interview mastery. From understanding the hidden job market to positioning yourself as a "Chief Marketing Officer" of your personal brand, the book equips you with the tools to take control of your career journey.

Each chapter blends expert guidance with interactive exercises, case studies, and tips to help you build a job search strategy that reflects your unique strengths and aspirations. With a special focus on overcoming modern hiring challenges like Applicant Tracking Systems (ATS) and virtual interviews, this book is both comprehensive and refreshingly user-friendly.

*Ace Your Job Search* is more than just a manual, it's a career empowerment guide designed to help you unlock your full potential, land your dream job, and build a future aligned with your goals and values.

# Acknowledgments

This journey began in 2002, when Shawn Mintz believed in me and encouraged me to lead a workshop for his clients at ACCES Employment. That first opportunity sparked something powerful in me. I remain deeply grateful to the late Arlene Insch (ex-Registrar, Human Resources Professionals Association (HRPA)), whose warm encouragement and kind spirit made that moment possible. Arlene was one of the first to see potential in me as a facilitator and encouraged me to write this book. Her quiet support gave me the confidence to begin, and her memory continues to inspire me.

Over the past two decades, I've had the privilege of guiding and learning from students, newcomers to Canada, mid-career professionals, and senior leaders. Each interaction has shaped me and contributed to this body of work, filling my journey with purpose, meaning, and continuous growth.

To everyone who has walked alongside me, thank you.

Your trust, encouragement, and thoughtful feedback have shaped both this book and the work that underpins it. I'm especially grateful to those who reviewed this workbook and shared their insights, helping bring clarity and impact to its pages. I would like to thank the following book reviewers: Amitabh Dubey, Belinda Gonzalez, Enza Ruscillo, Jessica Scarbeau, Lalitha Raavi, Licinia Neves, Magdalene Graham, Mehnaz Singh, Mira Toutounji, Ramneet Brar, Shawn Mintz and Rudinov Vincent.

To my dear friend, guide, and mentor Stephen White—thank you for your unwavering support and belief in me throughout every stage of this journey. Your presence has been a constant source of strength and encouragement.

To my wife, Vrushali—thank you for being my rock. Your love, patience, and belief in me have sustained me through it all. And to my daughters, Shreya and Sanjita—your pride and joy light up my world. You are my greatest motivation.

Finally, I dedicate this book to the memory of my late parents. They taught me the importance of kindness, hard work, and giving back. Their values are the foundation of everything I do, and I hope this book honors the legacy they left behind.

# Praise for – Ace Your Job Search

*"Sujay's book equips job seekers with the mindset, motivation, and strategies needed to stay proactive throughout their search. It's a must-read for anyone looking to fast-track their success—not just in landing the right job, but in thriving once they're there."*

*Shawn Mintz, President, MentorCity*

*"Ace Your Job Search is both insightful and actionable, exactly what today's job seekers need. Sujay brings operational clarity to a complex process, helping individuals position themselves strategically and confidently. This book doesn't just prepare you to get hired, it prepares you to thrive from day one."*

*Ramneet Brar, Chief Operating Officer, Wayable*

*"Sujay's Ace Your Job Search is a true game-changer. It reinforces a powerful truth: success requires both the right strategy and the right mindset. By focusing on resilience, adaptability, and continuous learning, Sujay shows readers how to turn rejection into a stepping stone. I especially appreciated the practical, step-by-step guidance, from tailoring your profile to standing out among hundreds of applicants and presenting yourself with impact. If you want to go from one of many to the one they hire, this book shows you how."*

*Rudinov Vincent, Founder & CEO, DIFEST GLOBAL - Diversity Inclusion Festival.*

*"This workbook strikes the perfect balance between strategy and practicality. It gives job seekers tools they can actually use, grounded in what employers are looking for today. Whether someone is re-entering the workforce, pivoting careers, or entering the job market for the first time, this resource helps them show up with clarity and confidence."*

*Mehnaz Singh, HR Generalist, Pivotal Integrated HR Solutions*

*"Are you ready to transform your career journey? Sujay's book provides a comprehensive roadmap for individuals exploring new opportunities. It's equipped with step-by-step guidelines to help you ace your dream job. I highly recommend it to anyone seeking complete guidance on job search strategy."*

*Lalitha Raavi, Senior Talent Acquisition Consultant, Gore Mutual Insurance*

*"Ace Your Job Search is a clear, practical guide to career success. The content not only outlines how to navigate the job search process but also includes relevant, up-to-date strategies for North American interview practices. It goes beyond simply landing a job, it helps individuals align with long-term career goals. A must-have for anyone serious about shaping their professional future."*

*Magdalene Graham, Human Resources Administrator, Peterborough Victoria Northumberland and Clarington Catholic District School Board*

# Contents

**INTRODUCTION** ........................................................................................................ 1
   The Job Search Success Formula ............................................................................. 1
   Mindset Matters – Step into the Role of CMO .......................................................... 2
   How to Use This Workbook ...................................................................................... 3

**Part I – Introspection & Self-Discovery** ................................................................. 7
   Understanding Your Strengths and Values ............................................................... 8
   Identifying Your Ideal Job and Work Environment ................................................. 11
   Clarifying Your Unique Value Proposition .............................................................. 14

**Part II - Plan – Job Search Strategy and Goal Setting** ........................................ 18
   Setting SMART Job Search Goals ........................................................................... 19
   Understanding How the Job Market Works ............................................................ 22
   Researching Target Employers and Industries ........................................................ 25
   Job Interview Imperatives: Researching a Company ............................................... 27
   Building and Expanding Your Network ................................................................... 30
   Building Your Portfolio Bag .................................................................................... 34
   Plan Your Business-Formal Appearance for Interviews and Networking Events ...... 38

**Part III - Marketing – Resume, LinkedIn, References and Job Search Materials** ....... 41
   Crafting a Winning Resume .................................................................................... 42
   Understanding How ATS (Applicant Tracking Systems) Work ................................ 47
   Optimizing Your LinkedIn Profile ............................................................................ 51
   Open to Work Settings (Job Seekers' Secret Weapon) ............................................ 53
   Writing a compelling cover ..................................................................................... 51
   Preparing Your References The Unsung Heroes of Your Job Search ....................... 58

**Part IV - Action – Job Applications, Interviews and Follow-Ups** ........................ 62
   Measuring Your Efforts: The 3000-Point Rule ......................................................... 63
   Exercise: Job Search Effort Tracker ......................................................................... 64
   Job Application Strategies and Tracking Progress ................................................... 66

Mastering Interviews and Storytelling .................................................................................. 68

Tips for Different Interview Formats ..................................................................................... 71

Negotiating Offers and Making Career Decisions ................................................................. 73

Case Study: Mastering Interviews and Negotiation .............................................................. 75

## Part V - Success – Staying Resilient and Sustaining Career Growth .......................... 76

Managing Job Search Stress and Staying Motivated ............................................................ 77

Thriving in Your New Role ..................................................................................................... 79

Gratitude: Your Secret Weapon for Career Success ............................................................ 82

Sample Thank-You Emails ..................................................................................................... 85

## Final Reflection and Next Steps ........................................................................................ 89

Key Takeaways and Lessons Learned .................................................................................... 90

Personal Job Search Commitment Statement ...................................................................... 91

Next Steps: Continuing Your Career Growth ........................................................................ 92

## Appendix ............................................................................................................................ 93

Tips for Unique Job Seekers .................................................................................................. 93

Resume Power Verbs by Category ....................................................................................... 107

# INTRODUCTION

*"Believe you can, and you are halfway there."* – Theodore Roosevelt

When confronted with rejection and uncertainty, the job search process can feel daunting. However, strategy, perseverance, and the correct mindset are more important for success than luck. This workbook is intended to serve as a manual to assist you in taking charge of your job search and securing your dream position.

*"The secret of getting ahead is getting started."* - Mark Twain

This workbook presents a structured framework for maintaining concentration and achieving quantifiable results, regardless of your background; you may be a fresh graduate, a mid-career professional looking for a change, someone returning to the field, re-entering the workforce after a hiatus or wanting to guide your mentee.

It adheres to the formula for a successful job search: I + Plan + Marketing + Action = Success. You will build a solid foundation, develop an engaging professional brand, and carry out a successful job search plan by segmenting the job search into five crucial stages.

## The Job Search Success Formula

Sending resumes and waiting for a response is only one aspect of a job search. A proactive and deliberate strategy is necessary. This workbook is intended to guide you through the following five crucial stages:

- **I - Self-Reflection - Knowing Yourself and Your Professional Objectives**: It's important to evaluate your goals, values, and strengths before applying for jobs. By taking this step, you can make sure that the chances you are pursuing fit with your long-term professional objectives.

- **Plan - Creating a Strategic Job Search Approach through Planning:** Searching for a job without a plan is like trying to drive without a map. Your chances of success will be greatly increased by establishing specific objectives, determining target employers, and conducting job market research, especially the hidden job market.

- **Marketing - Developing a Powerful Personal Brand, LinkedIn Profile, Resume and References:** Your cover letter, LinkedIn profile, and resume are your marketing collateral. They must be optimized for both recruiters and Applicant Tracking Systems (ATS) and provide a thought-provoking narrative about your qualifications and expertise. Equally important are your references—the often-unsung heroes of your job search. Cultivated thoughtfully, strong references can validate your achievements, reinforce your credibility, and give hiring managers the confidence to move forward with your candidacy.

- **Action - Effectively Applying, Networking, and Interviewing:** Applications are submitted in a single step. Your job search results will be greatly impacted by your strategic networking, interview **preparation**, and follow up with possible employers.

- **Success – Securing the Right Opportunity and Sustaining Momentum:** Success means landing a role that aligns with your values, goals, and strengths, not just accepting the first offer. A strong start in your new role sets the tone for long-term impact. Keep learning, stay connected, and reflect on your journey to guide future growth. And most importantly, express gratitude to those who supported you along the way. Gratitude not only strengthens relationships but also grounds you in humility and appreciation as you step into your next chapter.

## Mindset Matters – Step into the Role of CMO

No matter your profession or background, **you are now the Chief Marketing Officer (CMO) of your personal brand**. That means you need to think, act, and plan like a sales and marketing professional, not just the expert in your field looking for a job.

Looking for a job is your **new full-time, unpaid job**. Treat it like a 9-to-5 role. Show up daily with discipline, dressed professionally, focused, and ready to pitch your value.

Anyone who has worked in sales will tell you: **out of 100 calls, maybe 2 or 3 lead to a sale**. Rejection isn't personal, it's part of the game. Every "no" gets you one step closer to a "yes." Reframe rejection as progress.

To succeed:

- **Build a daily structure**: Work on your job search like a professional, set goals, track your activity, and stay consistent.
- **Dress the part**: Even if you're at home, show up for your job search like it's your job. This helps reinforce confidence and professionalism.
- **Adopt a learner's mindset**: Seek guidance, listen actively, make adjustments, and grow through feedback.
- **Focus on your personal growth**: Your only competition is who you were yesterday. Be a better version of yourself each day. Compete with yourself not others.
- **Drop the excuses**: Circumstances may not be ideal, but complaining won't change anything, and frankly, no one *else* cares. **You have to care enough to act.**

In short: Your mindset sets the tone for your entire job search. It's what fuels your energy, your approach, and ultimately, your success.

## How to Use This Workbook

This workbook is designed to help you through each stage of your job hunt. Following are some of the imperatives that the author deems necessary for the establishment of an excellent foundation:

- Finish worksheets to improve your confidence and lucidity.
- Track your progress and improve your strategy by using assessments.
- Go over portions again if necessary; the process of looking for a job is dynamic.

A great number of professionals have found success with the techniques presented in this workbook, whether in navigating career changes or securing roles that align with their strengths and goals. By applying these same strategies with focus and commitment, you'll be well-positioned to find a role that reflects your unique goals, values, and skill set.

*"Opportunities don't happen. You create them." - Chris Grosser*

## Let's take a look at a case study focused on an unsuccessful job search, and how it changed into a journey towards success

Alex, a seasoned professional in the middle of his career, found himself in an increasingly discouraging situation. After six months of relentless job searching with no success, he began to experience mounting frustration and self-doubt. Despite his extensive experience and qualifications, his efforts yielded little to no response from prospective employers. The constant stream of rejections eroded his confidence, leaving him disheartened and uncertain about his professional future.

Realizing that his approach was not yielding results, Alex took a step back to reassess his strategy. Instead of viewing job searching as a passive process dictated by external circumstances, he adopted a proactive mindset rooted in resilience and strategic planning. Drawing from the principles outlined in this workbook, he redefined his job search as a structured, goal-oriented endeavor. He established a disciplined routine, setting specific daily and weekly targets to maintain consistency. He shifted his perspective on rejection, no longer perceiving it as a personal failure but as a necessary step toward securing the right opportunity.

Beyond refining his approach, Alex actively sought ways to enhance his marketability. He revisited his professional branding materials, optimizing his resume and LinkedIn profile to better highlight his strengths. He also expanded his network by engaging in meaningful conversations with industry professionals, leveraging informational interviews and strategic connections to uncover hidden opportunities. With a renewed sense of purpose and direction, he remained persistent, applying his skills and experience with confidence.

As a result of his mindset shift and structured approach, Alex began to see tangible progress. Within three months, he received multiple interview invitations from reputable organizations. His preparation, confidence, and strategic follow-ups distinguished him as a strong candidate. Ultimately, he secured a leadership role at a company that not only valued his expertise but also aligned with his long-term career aspirations.

Alex's journey underscores the critical role that mindset plays in the job search process. By adapting resilience, maintaining discipline, and approaching challenges with a growth-oriented perspective, job seekers can revolutionize setbacks into stepping stones towards success.

## Self-Assessment: Where Are You Now?

Before proceeding with job applications, it's crucial to assess and scrutinize your current state. Here is a small self-assessment exercise to get you started:

*Rate yourself between 1-5, with 1 being needs work and 5 being strong, in the following areas:*

|  | 1 | 2 | 3 | 4 | 5 |
|---|---|---|---|---|---|
| Clarity on career goals | ☐ | ☐ | ☐ | ☐ | ☐ |
| Resume effectiveness | ☐ | ☐ | ☐ | ☐ | ☐ |
| LinkedIn profile strength | ☐ | ☐ | ☐ | ☐ | ☐ |
| Networking & referrals | ☐ | ☐ | ☐ | ☐ | ☐ |
| Interview preparation | ☐ | ☐ | ☐ | ☐ | ☐ |
| Confidence in job search | ☐ | ☐ | ☐ | ☐ | ☐ |
| Mindset | ☐ | ☐ | ☐ | ☐ | ☐ |

**Important Tip:** Please be honest with your self-reflection. I've seen individuals fail at this part as they try to say they have strengths they don't possess, as they think it's bad not to have certain strengths. They almost work to convince themselves they have these skills. Getting a true understanding of ones' careers goals starts with being honest with oneself.

## Reflection Questions

1. What are your top strengths in your job search?

   _____

   _____

   _____

2. Which areas need the most improvement?

   _____

   _____

   _____

3. What immediate steps can you take to strengthen your areas of growth?

   _____

   _____

   _____

# Part I – Introspection & Self-Discovery

*"The only way to do great work is to love what you do. If you haven't found it yet, keep looking. Don't settle." – Steve Jobs*

Before you start applying for jobs, it is pivotal to understand the following: Who Are You, What Do You Want, and What Makes You Unique?

Many job seekers jump straight into the application process without having a clear direction, which can lead to inevitable frustration and wasted effort. The ensuing section will help you with:

- Recognize your strengths, skills, and values
- Define your ideal job and work environment
- Shape a strong personal brand that sets you apart

# Understanding Your Strengths and Values

*"Knowing yourself is the beginning of all wisdom." – Aristotle*

Being familiar with your strengths and values will guide you towards roles that perfectly align with your skills and aspirations. Employers search for candidates who are not only equipped with the right skills but also share the company's values and culture.

*"What lies behind us and what lies before us are tiny matters compared to what lies within us."*
*- Ralph Waldo Emerson*

### Exercise: Self-Reflection on Career Goals

Take a deep breath and spare a few moments to reflect and answer the following questions:

- What type of work energizes you?

  _____
  _____

- What are the three things you have done in your career that you are most proud of?

  _____
  _____

- What are your top three professional strengths?

  _____
  _____

- What tasks or responsibilities do you enjoy the most in a job?

  _____
  _____

- What work environments (structured, flexible, remote, hybrid, fast-paced, collaborative, independent) suit you best?

  _____
  _____

*"Someone else's opinion of you does not have to become your reality."* - Les Brown

> **Tip**: Think about the times when you felt most engaged or fulfilled at work. What were you doing when such sensations paid you a visit; what made it meaningful?

## Assessment: Strengths and Skills Inventory

Use the table below to assess your strengths. Check the skills that best describe you:

| Skill Category | Strongest Skills | Skills to Improve |
|---|---|---|
| Problem-Solving | ☐ | ☐ |
| Leadership | ☐ | ☐ |
| Communication | ☐ | ☐ |
| Analytical Thinking | ☐ | ☐ |
| Creativity | ☐ | ☐ |
| Team Collaboration | ☐ | ☐ |
| Adaptability | ☐ | ☐ |
| Technical/Industry-Specific Skills | ☐ | ☐ |

## Reflection Questions

- Which three skills of yours, according to you, are the strongest?

  _____
  _____

- Which skills do you wish to improve upon?

  _____
  _____

- How can you leverage your strengths in your job search?

  _____
  _____

# Identifying Your Ideal Job and Work Environment

*"Find a job you enjoy doing, and you will never have to work a day in your life."* - Mark Twain

Before you set out to find the right job, ask yourself: **What am I looking for?**

The following exercise will help you determine your ideal job, industry, and work setting.

## Defining Your Dream Job

Fill in the blanks to create a vision of your ideal job:

"I want to work as a _____ *(job title)* in _____ *(industry/company type)* where I can use my skills in _____ *(key strengths)* to _____ *(contribute to specific goals)*. I thrive in a _____ *(work environment: remote, hybrid, office, team-based, independent)* setting, and I value _____ *(company culture aspects: innovation, stability, flexibility, growth opportunities, etc.).*"

## Sample Answer

*"I want to work as a Marketing Manager in the technology industry where I can use my skills in content creation and strategic planning to drive brand growth. I thrive in a collaborative and flexible environment, and I value companies that encourage creativity and professional development."*

## Assessment: Career Values Checklist

Which of the following values are most important to you in a job? (Check your top 5)

- ☐ Work-Life Balance
- ☐ Job Stability
- ☐ Growth Opportunities
- ☐ Leadership Opportunities
- ☐ Innovation & Creativity
- ☐ Financial Rewards

- [ ] Helping Others
- [ ] Autonomy & Independence
- [ ] Diversity & Inclusion
- [ ] Challenging Work
- [ ] Work Culture & Team Collaboration
- [ ] Company provided training

## Reflection Questions

- How do your values align with your past work experiences?

  _____
  _____
  _____

- Have you ever been in a job that didn't match your values? What was the result?

  _____
  _____
  _____

- What are three deal-breakers in your job search? (For me it has always been Autonomy, mastery & growth)

  _____
  _____
  _____

**Tip:** If a job doesn't align with your values, it may not be the right fit, no matter how good it looks on paper. In short, never settle for less. The sky should never be the limit…but the beginning.

## Case Study: Finding Career Clarity

**Situation:** David, a software engineer, felt stuck in his career but didn't know what he really wanted.

**Approach:** Using the workbook's *self-reflection exercises*, he identified his top values: growth, innovation, and work-life balance. He realized he wanted to move into AI development rather than stay in traditional coding roles.

**Outcome:** After aligning his job search with his values, he landed a new role in AI development with a flexible work arrangement.

*"Success is getting what you want. Happiness is wanting what you get."* - Dale Carnegie

# Clarifying Your Unique Value Proposition

*"Be yourself; everyone else is already taken."* - Oscar Wilde

Your Unique Value Proposition (UVP) is what sets you apart from other candidates. It is a concise statement that defines not just as a candidate but as a valuable potential resource and partner.

- Who you are?
- What you do best?
- How would you create value for an employer?

*"Do what you do so well that they will want to see it again and bring their friends."* - Walt Disney

### Exercise: Molding Your Personal Brand Statement

Use the formula below to write your UVP:

"I help [target audience] achieve [goal] by leveraging my expertise in [skills/industry]."

### Examples of Personal Brand Statements

*"I help startups scale their marketing efforts by leveraging my expertise in digital strategy and content creation."*

*"I improve employee engagement and retention for companies by applying my HR leadership and training expertise."*

*"I drive revenue growth for SaaS companies through data-driven sales strategies and relationship management."*

## Your Turn

Write your personal brand statement below:

*"I help _____ achieve _____ by leveraging my expertise in _____."*

**Tip:** This is the most important one-liner you'll use to introduce yourself. Whether you think best by speaking or writing, keep refining your Unique Value Proposition (UVP) until it clearly and confidently reflects who you are. Revisit and revise it as often as needed to ensure it aligns with your true strengths and purpose.

## Assessment: SWOT Analysis for Job Seekers

Complete the Strengths, Weaknesses, Opportunities and Threats SWOT analysis below to understand your competitive advantage:

Strengths (What do you do well?)

1. _____

2. _____

3. _____

Weaknesses (What could be improved?)

1. _____

2. _____

3. _____

Opportunities (What trends, networks, or skills can you leverage?)

1. _____

2. _____

3. _____

Threats (What challenges or obstacles exist in your job search?)

1. _____

2. _____

3. _____

## Reflection Questions

- What strengths make you a great candidate?

_____
_____
_____

- How can you overcome your weaknesses?

_____
_____
_____

- What new opportunities should you explore?

_____
_____
_____

> **Tip:** Use your SWOT insights to refine your resume, LinkedIn, and interview responses. Treat your insights like a chef treats their dish(es). Make them tasty, not just for yourself, but for the people who are going to review the aforementioned documents and platform.

*"Your brand is what people say about you when you're not in the room."* - Jeff Bezos

## Key Takeaways from This Section

- Understanding your strengths, skills, and values helps you focus on the right opportunities.
- Defining your ideal job and work environment ensures you apply for the right roles.
- Clarifying your unique value proposition makes you stand out to employers.

## What's Next

Move on to the **Plan – Job Search Strategy** section to turn your insights into a clear job search action plan.

# Part II - Plan – Job Search Strategy and Goal Setting

*"Opportunities don't happen…you create them." – Chris Grosser*

A successful job search requires more than just sending out resumes, it requires a structured plan, clear goals, and strategic actions. This section will help you:

- Set SMART Goals for your job search
- Understand how the job market works and where opportunities exist
- Research and identify target employers
- Build and expand your professional network
- Begin Building Your Professional Portfolio Bag
- Plan Your Business-Formal Appearance for interviews and networking events

By the end of this section, you will have a clear roadmap for your job search.

*"Give me six hours to chop down a tree, and I will spend the first four sharpening the axe." – Abraham Lincoln*

# Setting SMART Job Search Goals

*"A goal without a plan is just a wish."* - Antoine de Saint-Exupéry

Without clear set goals, your job search can inevitably feel overwhelming and unstructured.

Using the **SMART** goal framework (*Specific, Measurable, Achievable, Relevant, and Time-bound*), you can create a job search plan that keeps you on track without deviations.

### Exercise: Creating an Actionable Job Search Plan

Answer the following questions to set clear job search goals:

1. What type of job are you looking for? (State the industry, role, location)

   _____
   _____

2. How many job applications will you send per week? (Rough estimation)

   _____
   _____

3. How many networking interactions (calls, messages, events) will you aim for weekly?

   _____
   _____

4. What skills do you need to improve, and how will you develop them?

   _____
   _____

5. When do you want to secure a new job?

   _____
   _____

## Assessment: Goal-Setting Worksheet

SMART Goal Criteria

**Specific** (What exactly do you want to achieve?)
_____
_____

**Measurable** (How will you track progress?)
_____
_____

**Achievable** (Is it realistic given your skills, experience, and market conditions?)
_____
_____

**Relevant** (How does this align with your career objectives?)
_____
_____

**Time-bound** (What is your estimated deadline?)
_____
_____

*"You miss 100% of the shots you don't take." - Wayne Gretzky*

## SMART Goal

"I will apply to at least 5 targeted jobs per week, attend 2 networking events monthly, and have 3 informational interviews per month to expand my industry connections and increase my chances of landing a job within the next 3 months."

**Tip:** Regularly review and adjust your goals based on feedback(s) and progress.

# Understanding How the Job Market Works

*"Opportunities multiply as they are seized."* - Sun Tzu

The job market consists of *three layers*, and understanding them will help you maximize opportunities:

## The Three Job Markets

**Visible Job Market (20%)**: Jobs publicly advertised on job boards, company websites, LinkedIn, and recruiter postings. Apply through company websites, revamp resumes for ATS, and follow up with recruiters.

**Hidden Job Market (60%)**: Jobs that never get publicly posted; filled through internal referrals and networking. Network actively, attend industry events, and engage in informational interviews.

**Created Job Market (20%)**: Opportunities that don't exist yet but can be *created* by proactive professionals through networking and positioning themselves as valuable assets. Pitch your skills to companies, propose solutions to potential employers, and engage in thought leadership (e.g., LinkedIn posts).

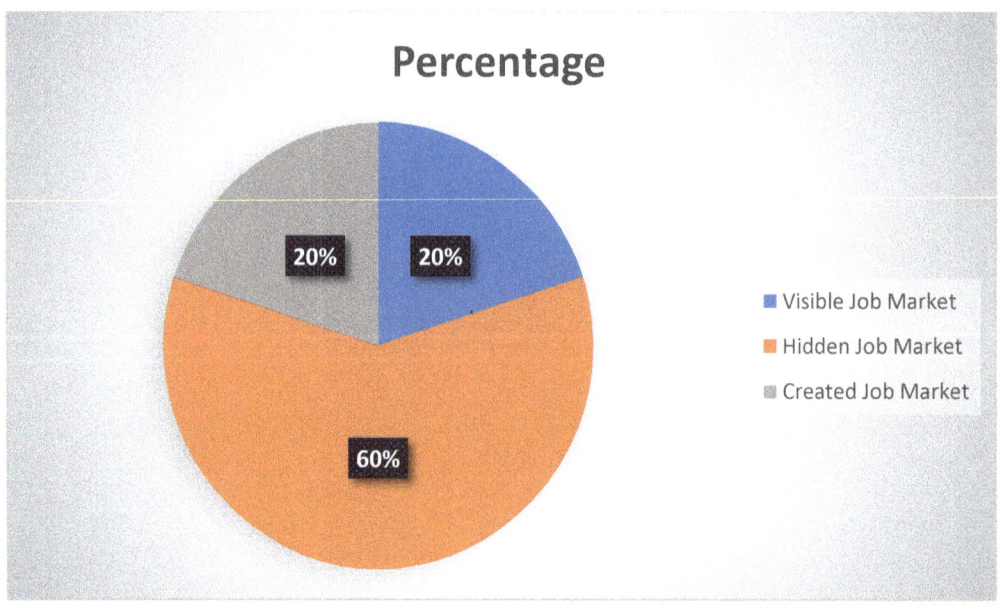

Adapted from Bolles, R. N. (2019). What Color Is Your Parachute? A Practical Manual for Job-Hunters and Career-Changers. Ten Speed Press; Lees, J. (2019). How to Get a Job You'll Love. McGraw-Hill; and Graham, D. (2018). Switchers: How Smart Professionals Change Careers and Seize Success. HarperCollins.

## Testimonial

*"I never knew how important the hidden job market was. After learning how to network strategically and tap into unadvertised opportunities, I landed a great role that wasn't even posted."* - Daniel P., Business Analyst

## Exercise: Mapping Your Opportunities

List potential job leads under each category:

| Visible Market | Hidden Market | Created Market |
|---|---|---|
| Job boards, LinkedIn, company career pages | Referrals, networking, recruiters | Direct outreach, freelance/contract work, project-based roles |
| | | |
| | | |
| | | |
| | | |
| | | |
| | | |
| | | |
| | | |

> **Tip:** Your ideal time allocation should be *20%* applying online and *80% networking & building relationships.*

*"Luck is what happens when preparation meets opportunity." - Seneca*

## Assessment: Identifying Your Best Market Entry Points

- Which market have you been focusing on the most?
- What steps can you take to tap into the hidden and created job markets?
- List three new networking strategies you will implement.

## Case Study: Tapping the Hidden Job Market

**Situation:** Priya, an operations manager, applied to over 100 jobs with no luck.

**Approach:** She used the workbook to create a *SMART job search plan* and focus on networking. Instead of relying solely on online applications, she reached out to past colleagues and joined industry groups.

**Outcome:** Through a connection, she discovered a role before it was posted and was hired within weeks.

# Researching Target Employers and Industries

*"Do your homework, and the world opens doors for you." - Oprah Winfrey*

Applying randomly to jobs is inefficient. Instead, *target specific employers* and research their industry trends.

**Tip:** Consider companies that have received Employer of Choice Awards (Great Place To Work, Aon Hewitt Best Employers Award, Fortune's World's Most Admired Companies etc.)

Identify around 5 industries and select 5-10 companies in each industry that align with your career goals.

| Target Company | Industry | Why This Company? (Values, Growth, Culture, etc.) | Hiring Contacts |
|---|---|---|---|
| Example: Google | Tech | Innovation, strong career growth | Recruiter/Department Manager: [Name] |
|  |  |  |  |
|  |  |  |  |
|  |  |  |  |
|  |  |  |  |
|  |  |  |  |
|  |  |  |  |
|  |  |  |  |

| | | | |
|---|---|---|---|
| | | | |
| | | | |
| | | | |
| | | | |
| | | | |
| | | | |
| | | | |
| | | | |
| | | | |
| | | | |
| | | | |
| | | | |
| | | | |

*"The future belongs to those who prepare for it today."* - Malcolm X

# Job Interview Imperatives: Researching a Company

1. Start with the Company Website
- **About / Mission & Values**: Understand their purpose, vision, and culture.
- **Leadership Team**: Know who runs the company, CEOs, department heads, etc.
- **Products/Services**: Know what they sell or offer. Be familiar with their core business.
- **News or Press Room**: Look for recent announcements, awards, partnerships, or expansion.
- **Careers Page**: Learn about their workplace culture, benefits, and internal initiatives.

2. Explore LinkedIn & Social Media
- **Company LinkedIn Page**:
    - Check updates, recent posts, and follower count.
    - Look at employee profiles to see their backgrounds and tenure.
- **Instagram / Facebook / Twitter / YouTube**:
    - Become familiar with company culture, events, and branding tone.
    - Look for videos or posts that offer insights into their values and internal life.

3. Use Glassdoor & Indeed Reviews
- Read employee reviews to understand:
    - Company culture
    - Work-life balance
    - Compensation trends
    - Interview experiences

*Be discerning, look for patterns rather than isolated comments.*

4. Google News Search
- Type: *Company Name + News*
    - Look for recent headlines, press coverage, or industry mentions.

5. Review Financials (if applicable)
- For public companies, check:
    - Annual Reports on the company website
    - Revenue, profitability, and growth areas

   - o Analyst ratings (Yahoo Finance, Morningstar)
- If it's a nonprofit or startup, look for impact reports, funding rounds, or donor profiles.

## 6. Understand the Industry & Competitors
- Get a sense of:
   - o The industry landscape
   - o Competitors and differentiators
   - o Trends and challenges affecting the sector

## 7. Research the Interviewers (if known)
- Look them up on LinkedIn:
   - o Know their role and background
   - o Look for shared connections or interests
   - o Helps you personalize your questions or small talk

## 8. Look into Company Culture & DEI Initiatives
- Check if they mention:
   - o DEI (Diversity, Equity, Inclusion) policies
   - o Employee resource groups
   - o Social impact programs

## 9. Firsthand Experience & Networking
- Connect with current and former employees via LinkedIn or alumni networks.
- If it's a retailer, visit one of their stores as a mystery shopper.
- Visit their plant, warehouse, vendors, suppliers, or stockists (if applicable).
- Observe customer service, store layout, branding, and frontline staff interaction.
- Gather direct insights to better understand their operational environment and customer experience.

**Bonus: Use What You Learn to Prepare**

**Why do you want to work here?** → Reference culture, values, or specific projects.

**What do you know about us?** → Mention recent news or product launches.

- What you want to know more about? Prepare a list of questions to ask at the end of the interview

## Assessment: Industry and Role Fit Analysis

Analyze the industries and roles you are interested in:

| Industry | Growth Trends | Required Skills | Best Fit for Me? (Yes/No) |
|---|---|---|---|
| Tech | AI, cybersecurity growth | Data analysis, problem-solving | Yes |
| Healthcare | Digital transformation | Patient care, project management | No |
| | | | |
| | | | |
| | | | |
| | | | |
| | | | |
| | | | |
| | | | |
| | | | |
| | | | |

**Tip:** Follow companies on LinkedIn, engage with their content, and attend webinars to stay visible.

# Building and Expanding Your Network

*"Your network is your net worth." - Porter Gale*

Networking is the *most effective job search strategy*. Over *80% of jobs* are filled through connections.

### Exercise: Mapping Your Professional Network

List people you can reach out to in different categories:

| Category | How Can They Help? | Next Step |
| --- | --- | --- |
| Friends & Family | Word-of-mouth job leads, moral support | Share job search goals |
| College & University Alumni | Works at a target company | Connect on LinkedIn |
| Professors/Mentors | Academic references, research roles | Email to request a meeting |
| Online Course Peers | Peer learning, job tips | Engage in course forums/discussions |
| Conference Contacts | New industry trends, peer introductions | Follow up via email |
| Internship & Coop Colleagues & Supervisors | Entry-level job leads, mentorship | Update on current status |
| Former Colleagues | Industry insights, referrals | Schedule a catch-up call |
| Former Bosses | Strong reference, leadership endorsement | Request reference or advice call |

| Industry Groups | Job leads, mentorship | Attend monthly meetup |
|---|---|---|
| Professional Associations | Access to exclusive job boards and certifications | Renew membership and attend events |
| Career Coaches | Resume review, mock interviews | Book a consultation |
| LinkedIn Connections | Works in desired role/field | Send personalized message |
| Volunteering Contacts | Nonprofit sector connections | Reconnect and explore opportunities |
| Recruiters/Head-hunters | Matchmaking with open roles | Reach out with updated resume |
| Hiring Managers | Direct job opportunities | Send resume with brief pitch |
| Doctors, Dentist, Hair Dressers, Beautician, Car driving instructor | Connect you to clients who work in your targeted companies | Inform them about your targeted companies and see if any of their clients work there |

*"Surround yourself only with people who are going to lift you higher." - Oprah Winfrey*

| Category | Name | How Can They Help? | Next Step |
|---|---|---|---|
| Friends & Family | | | |

| | | | |
|---|---|---|---|
| College & University Alumni | | | |
| Professors/Mentors | | | |
| Online Course Peers | | | |
| Conference Contacts | | | |
| Internship & Coop Colleagues & Supervisors | | | |
| Former Colleagues | | | |
| Former Bosses | | | |
| Industry Groups | | | |
| Professional Associations | | | |
| Career Coaches | | | |
| LinkedIn Connections | | | |
| Volunteering Contacts | | | |
| Recruiters/Head-hunters | | | |
| Hiring Managers | | | |
| Doctors, Dentist, Hair Dressers, Beautician, Car driving instructor | | | |

## Assessment: Networking Strength Assessment

Rate yourself on the following:

| Networking Skill | 1 (Needs Work) | 2 | 3 | 4 | 5 (Strong) |
|---|---|---|---|---|---|
| Reaching out to new contacts | ☐ | ☐ | ☐ | ☐ | ☐ |
| Engaging on LinkedIn | ☐ | ☐ | ☐ | ☐ | ☐ |
| Attending events and webinars | ☐ | ☐ | ☐ | ☐ | ☐ |
| Following up with connections | ☐ | ☐ | ☐ | ☐ | ☐ |

*"The richest people in the world look for and build networks. Everyone else looks for work."*
*- Robert Kiyosaki*

**Tip:** Focus on building genuine relationships, not just asking for jobs.

# Building Your Portfolio Bag

*"Your brand is a story unfolding across all customer touchpoints."* - Jonah Sachs

In today's competitive job market, a strong resume alone is not enough. A well-organized **Portfolio Bag** serves as your **professional narrative**, showcasing not just what you've done, but how well you've done it, and the value you bring.

Think of your portfolio as your **career passport**, a powerful tool that communicates your skills, achievements, learning journey, and character at a glance.

*"Success is where preparation and opportunity meet."* - Bobby Unser

Whether you're attending an interview, meeting a mentor, or preparing for performance discussions, your portfolio is your silent advocate, reflecting your **commitment, credibility, and consistency**.

In this section, you will learn:

- What to include in a compelling portfolio
- How to structure it effectively
- Tips to personalize and enhance your brand presence

Get ready to build a portfolio that doesn't just say "I can do the job," but rather, **"I'm the best person for the job."**

## Portfolio Binder Sections

### Section 1: Cover Page

- Full Name
- Professional Title / Tagline
- Contact Info
- Professional photo (optional)

## Section 2: Table of Contents

- Clickable list of sections (hyperlinked if digital)

## Section 3: Career Summary / Personal Brand Statement

- 2–3 paragraphs telling your professional story
- Keywords that reflect your brand

## Section 4: Cover Letter

- Tailored for the role or opportunity
- Include date, recipient, intro, body, and closing

## Section 5: Resume Snapshot

- Clean resume view or summary highlights
- Option to link to full resume (PDF)

## Section 6: Educational Certificates

- List with thumbnails of certificates (clickable or expandable)
- Include institution, year, and relevance
- If education is overseas provide credential evaluation and Equivalency

## Section 7: Professional Development & Training

- Table or infographic of courses, workshops, seminars, licenses

## Section 8: Self-Assessments

- Strengths summary or visuals from Myers–Briggs Type Indicator (MBTI), Dominance, influence, Steadiness, and Conscientiousness (DISC), etc.
- Personal reflection or growth takeaway

## Section 9: Work Samples / Projects

- Use visuals/screenshots
- Include a brief project summary: *Challenge → Action → Result*

## Section 10: Performance Appraisals

- Key excerpts from past evaluations
- Highlighted quotes or ratings

## Section 11: Appreciation & Testimonials

- Screenshots/emails/notes from peers or clients
- Or quote-style layout with names and context

## Section 12: Reference Letters & Contacts

- List with names, roles, and contact info
- Attach letters or links to view/download

## Optional Add-On Sections

### Section 13: LinkedIn Profile Snapshot

- Include your LinkedIn profile link
- Include profile highlights
- Include stats (connections, endorsements)

### Section 14: Leadership Philosophy / Work Ethic / Teaching Philosophy

- One paragraph professional philosophy
- Visuals or icons can help here

### Section 15: Volunteer & Community Work

- Describe roles, causes, outcomes

### Section 16: Strategic Projects / Impact Stories

- Case study-style layout (Situation, Task, Action, Results – STAR) or (Challenge, Action, Result- CAR format)

## Section 17: Professional Affiliations

- Logos of associations + "Member since [year]"

## Section 18: Future Goals & Development Plan

- Timeline or vision board style layout

## Section 19: DEI Contributions

- Summarize efforts, roles in ERGs, inclusive hiring, etc.

## Section 20: Digital Portfolios

- In creative, tech, or freelance industries, personal websites and digital portfolios are increasingly critical. Provide a list of your digital presence (e.g., Wix, Squarespace, GitHub, Notion).

## Section 21: Closing / Final Thoughts

- Thank you note
- Call to action (e.g., "Let's connect")
- Contact details again

# Plan Your Business-Formal Appearance for Interviews and Networking Events

Your appearance speaks volumes before you even say a word. In today's competitive job market, dressing appropriately in business-formal attire is not just about looking good, it's about communicating professionalism, preparedness, and respect for the opportunity. Whether you're attending a job interview or a networking event, how you present yourself can influence perceptions and build credibility.

Business-formal attire typically includes tailored suits, professional shoes, minimal accessories, and well-groomed hair. It's important to research the company culture ahead of time and dress slightly more formally than their day-to-day norm. When in doubt, lean toward classic, neutral colors and timeless styles. Your outfit should enhance your confidence and ensure you feel comfortable, focused, and ready to make a lasting impression.

Remember, your attire is an extension of your personal brand. Use it strategically to reflect your attention to detail, confidence, and readiness for the professional world.

*"Dress how you want to be addressed." - Bianca Frazier*

## Professional Dressing Checklist for Job Interviews

*(Check off each item as you prepare!)*

**General (For Everyone)**

☐ I have researched the company culture to determine whether I should dress in business formal or business casual attire.

☐ My clothing is clean, well-fitted, and wrinkle-free.

☐ I am wearing neutral or muted colors (e.g., navy, black, gray, beige, or white).

☐ My grooming is professional (hair styled neatly, nails clean and trimmed, minimal or no fragrance).

☐ My accessories are minimal and professional (no flashy or noisy items).

## For Men

**Business Formal**

☐ I am wearing a two-piece suit in navy, black, or gray.

☐ My dress shirt is crisp, collared, and white or light-colored.

☐ I have chosen a simple, solid-colored, or subtly patterned tie.

☐ My dress shoes are polished and either black or brown.

☐ I am wearing dark socks that match my suit (not white or athletic socks).

☐ My belt matches my shoes.

**Business Casual**

☐ I am wearing a blazer or sport coat with slacks or chinos.

☐ My shirt is a button-down or collared polo, tucked in.

☐ My shoes are loafers, brogues, or oxfords (no sneakers).

☐ I have added a simple accessory, like a watch, and a leather belt.

## For Women

**Business Formal**

☐ I am wearing a tailored pantsuit, skirt suit, or a formal dress with a blazer.

☐ My blouse or shirt is neutral-colored and professional (not low-cut or casual).

☐ My skirt or dress is knee-length or longer.

☐ My shoes are closed-toe pumps or flats in a neutral tone.

☐ I am wearing nude or black stockings (if opting for a skirt or dress).

**Business Casual**

☐ I am wearing a blazer with slacks, a skirt, or a simple dress.

☐ My top is a collared shirt, blouse, or sweater.

☐ My bottoms are slacks, chinos, or a knee-length skirt.

☐ My shoes are flats, loafers, or low-heeled shoes. (If open-toe, they are conservative and polished.)

## Final Touches (For Everyone)

☐ My hair is neatly styled and professional (avoiding elaborate hairstyles).

☐ My nails are clean and trimmed (neutral or subtle nail polish is applied if used).

☐ My jewelry is minimal (e.g., a watch, stud earrings, or a simple bracelet).

☐ I am carrying a professional-looking portfolio, briefcase, or tote bag (no casual backpacks).

## Industry-Specific Adjustments

☐ **Tech/Creative Fields**: I have opted for business casual attire (e.g., smart blazer, button-down shirt with dark jeans or chinos).

☐ **Startups/Small Businesses**: I researched the company's culture and chose business casual, which feels appropriate.

## Key Reminder

☐ I feel confident, comfortable, and professional in my outfit.

☐ My attire reflects respect for the opportunity and demonstrates my seriousness about the role.

## Key Takeaways from This Section

- Set *SMART Goals* to stay focused.
- Understand the *hidden and created job markets* to unravel more opportunities.
- Research *target employers* to craft your applications and networking efforts.
- *Networking is key*, most jobs are filled through relationships.
- Begin Building Your Professional Portfolio Bag
- Plan Your Business-Formal Appearance for interviews and networking events

**What's Next ?**: Move on to *Marketing – Resume, LinkedIn & Personal Branding* to craft your application materials.

# Part III - Marketing – Resume, LinkedIn, Cover letter, References and Job Search Materials

*"Your résumé is a chance to tell the world why you're remarkable. Don't settle for anything less."*
*– Anonymous*

Your resume, LinkedIn profile, and cover letter are your *personal marketing tools* in the job search process. This section will help you craft insightful materials that showcase your skills, experience, and unique value proposition.

By the end of this section, you will:

- Have a polished, high-impact resume tailored for your target roles.
- Understand how ATS (Applicant Tracking Systems) work and how to optimize your resume.
- Build a LinkedIn profile that attracts recruiters and strengthens your professional brand.
- Write a compelling cover letter that makes a strong first impression.

# Crafting a Winning Resume

*"Your résumé is not just a list of jobs; it's your personal story of growth and achievement. Craft it with passion and purpose." - Unknown*

A resume is *your first impression*, it should be concise, well-structured, and molded according to each job application.

## Key Resume Guidelines

- Keep it one or two pages (unless applying for senior/executive roles).
- Use a clean, professional format with clear headings and bullet points.
- Focus on achievements rather than responsibilities.
- Use quantifiable results (e.g., "Increased sales by 20%" instead of "Responsible for sales") and use action verbs (suggested list provided)
- Shape your resume in order to include keywords from the job description.
- Refrain from having overly personal information available (i.e. unrelated hobbies, non-professional interests, birthdates, and profile pictures.)

## Exercise: Resume Self-Check

Review your current resume and answer the following questions:

1. Does my resume clearly reflect my target role?
2. Is it error-free and formatted professionally?
3. Have I used action verbs and quantified results?
4. Is it tailored to each job application?
5. Does it use buzzwords from the job ad?

*"Your resume is a reflection of your potential, make it count." - Unknown*

## Assessment: Resume Scorecard

| Resume Criteria | Strong (✓) | Needs Work (X) |
|---|---|---|
| Clear and professional format | | |
| Strong summary statement | | |
| Experience focusing on achievements, not duties | | |
| Uses quantifiable data where possible | | |
| Tailored for the specific job | | |

**Tip:** Ask a mentor or career coach to review your resume for feedback.

Suggested Resume Template – Feel free to customize

Full Name, Educational Credentials i.e. BSc, MS

Phone: [Your Phone Number]
Email: [Professional Email Address]
LinkedIn: [LinkedIn URL] (if available and up to date)
Location: [City, Province/State – Optional]

## 1. Professional Summary (Skills-Focused)

A concise 2–3 sentence summary showcasing your key skills, academic strengths, and career goals. Tailor this to highlight what you bring to a potential employer.

**Example:**
Detail-oriented and results-driven graduate with a strong academic background in [Your Field, e.g., Business/Engineering/IT]. Demonstrated ability to work collaboratively, solve complex problems, and adapt quickly to new environments. Passionate about contributing to [industry/sector] through continuous learning and impactful work.

## 2. Education

**[University/College Name]**
*Degree or Certificate Title (e.g., Bachelor of Science in Computer Science, Graduate Certificate in Marketing)*
Graduation Date: [Month, Year] (or Expected Graduation Date)
GPA: [Your GPA] (include if 3.5 or above)
Relevant Coursework: [List 4–6 relevant courses based on your major]
Honors/Awards: [Dean's List, Scholarships, etc.]

**[Previous Institution, if applicable]**
*Degree Title*
Graduation Date: [Month, Year]
GPA: [Your GPA] (include if 3.5 or above)

Relevant Coursework: [List courses relevant to your field]

Honors/Awards: [Any notable academic achievements]

> **Tip**: Education section is placed early in a resume for recent graduates, for someone who recently acquired a qualification with a purpose of switching careers. In most other cases the education section is placed latter in the resume

## 3. Skills

**Technical/Professional Skills:**

- [Skill 1: e.g., Data Analysis using Python]
- [Skill 2: e.g., Project Planning and Execution]
- [Skill 3: e.g., CAD Software | CRM Platforms | SQL]
- [Skill 4: e.g., Marketing Strategy | SEO Optimization]
- [Skill 5: Industry tools or technologies relevant to your field]

**Soft Skills:**

- Communication (Written & Verbal)
- Team Collaboration
- Problem-Solving
- Adaptability
- Time Management
- Critical Thinking
- Ethical Conduct and Confidentiality

## 4. Projects (Ideal for Students or Early-Career Professionals)

**Project Title** *(Bold)*

Brief Description: 1–2 sentence overview of project objective.

Role: [Your Role]

Key Contributions:

- [Responsibility/Achievement using action verbs – quantify impact if possible]
- [Skill(s) demonstrated or tools/technologies used]

- [Teamwork or leadership contribution if applicable]

*Example:* **Business Process Improvement Project**

Redesigned workflow for a simulated logistics firm to reduce delivery time inefficiencies.

Role: Team Lead

- Conducted root cause analysis using process mapping.
- Proposed and modeled new solutions using Microsoft Visio.
- Resulted in a projected 15% efficiency gain in simulated operations.

## 5. Experience (Internships, Part-Time Jobs, Volunteering)

**Job Title** | *Company Name* | [Start Date – End Date]

- [Describe tasks and accomplishments – highlight transferable skills]
- [Use action verbs: managed, created, analyzed, coordinated, etc.]
- [Mention software, tools, or methodologies used if applicable]

*Example:* **Customer Service Associate** | Retail Co. | Jan 2023 – Aug 2023

- Handled an average of 50+ customer inquiries per day, resolving issues with a 95% satisfaction rate.
- Trained 2 new employees on POS systems and customer engagement techniques.
- Maintained accurate transaction records with minimal errors (<1%).

## 6. Certifications / Professional Memberships (If applicable)

- [Certification Name] – [Issuing Body], [Month, Year]
- Member, [Professional Association Name], [Start Date – Present]

## 7. Awards and Recognition (Optional)

- [Award Title], [Institution/Organization], [Year]
- [Scholarship or Grant Name], [Year]

## 8. References

Available upon request.

# Understanding How ATS (Applicant Tracking Systems) Work

*"A well-optimized ATS friendly resume gets past the gatekeepers." – Sujaykumar Vardhmane*

## What is ATS?

Most companies use *Applicant Tracking Systems (ATS)* to screen resumes before a human ever sees them. These systems filter resumes based on keywords, formatting, and structure.

## How to Optimize for ATS

- Use standard resume formatting (avoid tables, columns, and graphics).
- Incorporate relevant keywords from the job description.
- Spell out acronyms (e.g., "Customer Relationship Management (CRM)").
- Use a Word or PDF format, based on employer preference.

## How to Make Your Resume ATS-Friendly

ATS use algorithms to parse/ filter through resumes. Your resume will be more effective when following the below tips

**Keyword Optimization:** ATS ranks resumes by keyword relevance, match your skills with job descriptions. Use exact phrasing from job postings (e.g., "Project Management" instead of "Managing Projects"). Avoid using filler words, stick to the facts.

**Header Formatting**

Use **standard section headings**:

- *Work Experience* (✔) → (*Career Story* ✘)
- *Education* (✔) → (*Academic Journey* ✘)
- *Skills* (✔) → (*My Professional Toolkit* ✘)

ATS struggles with tables, columns, text boxes, and fancy graphics, stick to simple formatting.

## Resume File Format

- Save as .docx (Word) for best ATS compatibility.

- Use PDF (only if specified), some ATS systems struggle with PDFs.

## Bullet Points vs. Paragraphs

- Use bullet points instead of large paragraphs for clarity and ATS parsing.

## Example

*ATS-Friendly Bullet Points (✔)*

- Managed $1M+ budget for marketing campaigns, increasing ROI by 30%.

- Led a team of 10 in product development, launching 3 new features in 6 months.

*Unfriendly Paragraphs (✘)*

"I was responsible for managing a large budget for marketing campaigns and leading a team in product development, where we successfully launched new features within a few months."

# ATS-Friendly vs. Unfriendly Resume Formats

*"Technology will never replace great people, but great people who embrace technology will replace those who don't." – Unknown*

*ATS-Friendly:*

- Standard fonts (*Arial, Calibri, Times New Roman, Verdana*).
- No images, logos, tables, or special characters.
- Clearly labeled sections with consistent formatting.

*Unfriendly:*

- Fancy fonts (*Script, Comic Sans, Decorative Styles*).
- Text inside tables, columns, or graphics (which ATS can't read).
- Missing job-relevant keywords.

**Exercise: Optimizing Your Resume for ATS**

1. Take a job description for your target role.
2. Highlight 5–10 key skills and keywords used repeatedly.
3. Ensure these keywords are naturally included in your resume.

## Assessment: ATS Compatibility Checklist

| ATS-Friendly Feature | Included? (✓/X) |
|---|---|
| • Uses standard headings (e.g., Work Experience, Education) | |
| • No images, tables, or complex formatting | |
| • Keywords from the job description are included | |
| • Correct file format (Word or ATS-compatible PDF) | |

**Tip:** Run your resume through Jobscan or Resume Worded for an ATS match score.

## Case Study: Beating the ATS and Enhancing Online Presence

**Situation:** Maria was submitting resumes but wasn't getting interviews.

**Approach:** She followed the **ATS optimization** checklist and improved her LinkedIn profile using the workbook. She added industry keywords, highlighted measurable achievements, and started engaging with posts in her field.

**Outcome:** Within two weeks, recruiters started reaching out, and she landed an interview that led to her new job.

# Optimizing Your LinkedIn Profile

*"Your LinkedIn profile is your digital handshake, make it strong." - Unknown*

Recruiters actively search for candidates on LinkedIn, so your profile should be searchable, engaging, and complete.

Use LinkedIn to network. Reach out and make connections with those in the industry, those working for companies you would like to work with

## Key LinkedIn Profile Optimizations

- Professional Profile Picture (High-quality, clear, and friendly).
- Banner Picture (related to industry or personalized banner)
- Compelling Headline (More than just your job title, highlight your expertise).
- Keyword-Rich Summary (Showcase your skills, experience, and value).
- Detailed Work Experience (Use resume bullet points and quantify achievements).
- Skills and Endorsements (List at least 10 relevant skills).
- Recommendations (Both received and given)
- Engagement (Post insights, comment on industry trends, and connect with professionals).

*"Brand yourself for the career you want, not the job you have." - Dan Schawbel*

### Exercise: LinkedIn Profile Checklist

| Profile Section | Completed? (✓/X) |
|---|---|
| Profile photo is professional and up to date | |
| Headline includes keywords & personal branding | |
| Summary highlights your value proposition | |
| Work experience uses achievement-focused bullet points | |
| At least 10+ skills listed and endorsed | |

## Assessment: LinkedIn Headline and Summary Review

Does your headline clearly convey your expertise? Example:

**Instead of:** "Marketing Manager"

**Try:** "Digital Marketing Expert | Helping Brands Grow Through SEO & Data-Driven Strategies"

**Tip:** Engage in LinkedIn networking by posting industry insights and commenting on relevant discussions.

## Testimonial

*"Once I optimized my resume for ATS and revamped my LinkedIn profile, I started getting calls from recruiters. I never realized how much these small tweaks could impact my job search."*

*- Jake M., Sales Director*

# Open to Work Settings
# (Job Seekers' Secret Weapon)

How to Enable Open to Work:

1. Go to Your LinkedIn Profile.
2. Click "Open to" button (below your headline).
3. Choose "Finding a new job".
4. Set preferences (job titles, locations, remote work, industries).
5. Choose who can see it:
    - Recruiters only (discreet option).
    - All LinkedIn members (publicly visible with a green "Open to Work" badge).
6. Click Save, recruiters will now see your profile in their searches.

## Publishing Articles and Engaging on LinkedIn

Step-by-Step Guide to Publishing an Article on LinkedIn:

1. Go to LinkedIn Home Page.
2. Click "Write an Article" under the post section.
3. Write about industry trends, job search experiences, or career advice.
4. Add hashtags (*#JobSearch #CareerGrowth*).
5. Click Publish.

## Why Does Engaging/ Posting Matter?

- Sharing articles & posts boosts visibility and positions you as a thought leader.
- Recruiters favor active, engaged professionals on LinkedIn.

## LinkedIn Profile Optimization Checklist

**Headline:** Clearly state your expertise (e.g., "Marketing Specialist | SEO & Digital Strategy").

## About Section:

- Write in first-person ("*I specialize in...*").
- Include keywords from your target job description.
- Showcase achievements, skills, and industry experience.

## Experience Section:

- Bullet-point key accomplishments.
- Include metrics (e.g., "Increased sales by 25% in 6 months").

## Skills & Endorsements:

- Add job-relevant skills and request endorsements from colleagues.
  Engagement:
- Comment on industry-related posts.
- Join LinkedIn groups relevant to your field.
- Connect with industry professionals (add a personalized message when sending a request).

# Case Study:
# How LinkedIn Optimization Led to a Dream Job

From Unnoticed to Multiple Job Offers in 30 Days

Meet Sandy – a Marketing Manager who had been job searching for 4 months with no results. Her LinkedIn was inactive, and she wasn't showing up in recruiter searches.

## Steps Sandy Took to Transform Her LinkedIn:

**Updated Headline:** Changed from *"Marketing Enthusiast"* → *"Digital Marketing Manager | SEO | Content Strategy | Growth Marketing"* (using industry keywords).

- Revamped Summary: Added achievements and personal brand statement.
- Skills & Endorsements: Added 10 relevant skills & asked colleagues to endorse.
- Engaged Weekly: Started commenting on industry posts and writing one article per week.
- Connected with Recruiters: Sent personalized connection requests to hiring managers.
- Enabled "Open to Work" (recruiter visibility).

**Results:** Within 30 days, Sandy got:

- 5x more profile views.
- 2 job offers from recruiters who found her profile.
- A marketing manager role with a $10K salary increase.

**Key Takeaway:** Optimizing LinkedIn isn't just about looking good, it's about making yourself discoverable to the right employers.

# Writing a Compelling Cover Letter

*"The cover letter is your elevator pitch—crafted for one person, with one purpose: to get the interview." — Unknown*

A cover letter is your chance to tell your career story, highlight key accomplishments, and explain why you're the right fit.

## Key Cover Letter Guidelines

- Address it to the hiring manager (if possible).
- Start with a strong opening (mention a connection or enthusiasm for the company).
- Highlight two or three key skills/achievements relevant to the job.
- End with a call to action (e.g., "I look forward to discussing how I can contribute.").
- Tailor each cover letter to the job posting.

## Exercise: Tailoring Your Cover Letter

1. Identify three key skills/achievements you want to emphasize.
2. Write a strong opening paragraph that captures attention.
3. Craft a closing statement that shows enthusiasm and invites a next step.

Example Cover Letter Opening:

"Dear [Hiring Manager's Name],
I was excited to come across the [Job Title] position at [Company Name]. With a background in [your expertise] and a passion for [industry-specific detail], I am eager to bring my skills in [relevant skill] to your team. In my previous role at [Previous Company], I [achievement with measurable impact]."

*"People don't hire resumes. They hire personality, purpose, and potential—your cover letter brings those to life." — Anonymous*

## Assessment: Cover Letter Effectiveness Rubric

| Cover Letter Element | Strong (✓) | Needs Work (X) |
|---|---|---|
| Strong opening paragraph | | |
| Highlights relevant skills & achievements | | |
| Tailored to the job and company | | |
| Ends with a clear call to action | | |

**Tip:** Keep it concise (1 page) and always customize it for each job.

# Preparing Your References
# The Unsung Heroes of Your Job Search

*"A reference is not just someone who speaks on your behalf—it's someone who believes in your potential." – Sujaykumar Vardhmane*

Strong references can be the tipping point between a job offer and a polite rejection. Many candidates underestimate their power. This chapter helps you strategically prepare, manage, and leverage references like a pro.

## Why References Matter

Employers use references to:

- Confirm your past performance and work ethic
- Gauge your reliability, integrity, and attitude
- Assess cultural fit and growth potential

A glowing reference doesn't just validate your resume—it strengthens your professional credibility.

## Who Should Be Your References?

Aim for 3–5 people who know your work ethic, skills, and character. Consider:

| Type | Ideal If... |
| --- | --- |
| Professors or Academic Advisors | You're a student or recent graduate, or did a thesis/project with them |
| Current/Former Bosses | You performed well and had a good working relationship |
| Clients or Vendors | You worked directly with them on deliverables or service quality |
| Colleagues or Peers | You collaborated regularly or led team projects together |
| Mentors | They've guided your professional development or career direction |

> **Tip:** Choose references who can speak to different facets of your skills—technical, interpersonal, leadership, and reliability.

## How to Ask Someone to Be a Reference

Be respectful, clear, and give context. Use this simple 3-step approach:

### 1. Ask Personally (Not by Text or Social Media DM)

Send an email or call them directly. Example:

"I'm in the process of applying for [Job Title] roles and would be honored if I could list you as a reference. You've seen my work on [Project/Role], and I value your perspective."

### 2. Explain Why You Chose Them

"You were my manager during a pivotal stage in my career, and your support made a big difference."

### 3. Give Them an Easy Out

"If this isn't a good time or you'd prefer not to, I completely understand."

## Cultivating the Relationship

Don't just reach out when you need something. Build ongoing goodwill:

- Send updates every few months: "Here's how my job search is going."
- Share professional wins or learning: "Just completed a data analytics course!"
- Offer value: Recommend a good article or congratulate them on a milestone.

Relationships grow with attention, not just requests.

## Keep Your References in the Loop

Before you give their name:

- **Confirm their contact info** and preferred method (email or phone)
- **Let them know about the role**: company, position, what the employer may ask
- **Send your resume and cover letter** so they know your narrative

Example Email:

**Subject:** Reference Request – [Your Name]

Hi [Name],

I wanted to thank you again for agreeing to be my reference. I've applied to a [Job Title] position at [Company], and I think your perspective on my work during [Project or Role] will be really valuable.

Attached is my updated resume and the job description. Please let me know if you'd like any more context. I appreciate your support so much!

Warm regards,

[Your Name]

## Exercise: Reference Readiness Tracker

| Name | Role | Relationship | Confirmed? (Y/N) | Last Thanked | Notes |
|------|------|--------------|------------------|--------------|-------|
|      |      |              |                  |              |       |
|      |      |              |                  |              |       |
|      |      |              |                  |              |       |

## Checklist: Reference Management

| Task | Done? |
|------|-------|
| Identified 3–5 strong references | ☐ |
| Contacted each with context and request | ☐ |
| Sent updated resume and job info | ☐ |
| Logged their details for quick access | ☐ |
| Sent thank-you message or follow-up | ☐ |

## Always Thank Your References

Whether you get the job or not, acknowledge their time and effort.

- Send a **thank-you note or email**
- Let them know the outcome of your applications
- Consider a small token of appreciation if appropriate (e.g., a coffee card, a professional book, a shoutout on LinkedIn)

**Example Thank-You Note:**

"Thank you for speaking on my behalf. I really appreciate your support and the time you took. Your words made a difference."

# Real Voices

*"I kept my references in the loop. One even gave me insider tips before my final interview. That edge helped me land the job." — Arjun M., Marketing Analyst*

## Final Reflection & Next Steps

Think of your references as trusted allies—not just a checkbox on a form. Invest in those relationships, keep them informed, and express sincere appreciation. When employers see that others believe in you, they'll be more likely to believe in you too.

## Key Takeaways from This Section

- A strong resume highlights achievements and is ATS-friendly.
- Your LinkedIn profile should be optimized and engaging to attract recruiters.
- A tailored cover letter makes you stand out by connecting your skills to the role.
- Thoughtfully chosen references are the unsung heroes of your job search—prepare, inform, and thank them for their support.

**What's Next?:** Move on to Action – Job Applications, Interviews & Follow-Ups.

# Part IV - Action – Job Applications, Interviews and Follow-Ups

*"Confidence comes from preparation. The more you prepare, the more confident you'll be." – Richard Branson*

Taking consistent and strategic action is where everything comes together. This section focuses on tracking efforts, applying effectively, excelling in interviews, and negotiating offers to ensure job search success.

By the end of this section, you will:

- Measure your job search progress using the 3000-Point Rule.
- Learn how to track applications, networking, and follow-ups for better results.
- Master interview techniques using the STAR Method and storytelling.
- Develop strategies for negotiating offers and making informed career decisions.

# Measuring Your Efforts: The 3000-Point Rule

*"Success is the sum of small efforts, repeated day in and day out." - Robert Collier*

Many job seekers underestimate the amount of effort required to secure a job. The 3000-Point Rule ensures that you're putting in enough strategic effort across multiple activities to maximize your chances of success.

## How It Works

Each job search activity has a point value, and your goal is to accumulate at least 3000 points every week.

**High-Impact Activities (100–200 points)**

- Attending a networking event – 100 points
- Meeting someone for an informational interview – 150 points
- Submitting a highly targeted application – 100 points
- Getting a job interview – 200 points

**Moderate-Impact Activities (50–100 points)**

- Following up on an application – 50 points
- Reaching out to a recruiter – 50 points
- Applying for a job with a general resume – 75 points

**Low-Impact Activities (10–50 points)**

- Updating your LinkedIn profile – 50 points
- Watching an interview preparation webinar – 25 points

**Rule of Thumb:** If you're consistently scoring UNDER 3000 points every week for 5-6 weeks, increase your networking and high-impact activities.

## Testimonial

*"Tracking my job search using the 3000-Point Rule helped me stay motivated. I realized I wasn't applying to enough quality roles or following up effectively. Once I did, interviews started coming in!" - Ethan L., Data Analyst*

# Exercise: Job Search Effort Tracker

Create a weekly log to track your activities and total points.

| Activity | Max Points | Earned Points | Remarks |
|---|---|---|---|
| High-Impact Activities (100–200 points) | | | |
| Attending a networking event | 100 points | | |
| Meeting someone for an informational interview | 150 points | | |
| Submitting a highly targeted application | 100 points | | |
| Getting a job interview | 200 points | | |
| Moderate-Impact Activities (50–100 points) | | | |
| Following up on an application | 50 points | | |
| Reaching out to a recruiter | 75 points | | |
| Applying for a job with a general resume | 50 points | | |

| Low-Impact Activities (10–50 points) | | | |
|---|---|---|---|
| Updating your LinkedIn profile | 50 points | | |
| Watching an interview preparation webinar | 25 points | | |

## Assessment: Are You Meeting Your Activity Targets?

- Have you accumulated at least 3000 points every week in the past 6 weeks?
- Are your activities diversified between networking, applications, and follow-ups?
- If you're not getting responses, are you adjusting your approach?

> **Tip:** Focus more on relationship-building and referrals rather than just online applications.

# Job Application Strategies and Tracking Progress

*"Success is where preparation and opportunity meet."* – Bobby Unser

A disorganized job search leads to missed opportunities and wasted efforts. Keeping track of your applications helps you follow up effectively and identify what's working.

## Best Practices for Job Applications

- Customize your resume & cover letter for each application.
- Apply through multiple channels (company website, referrals, recruiters).
- Keep a Job Application Tracker to track responses and follow-ups.

## Example of a Job Application Tracker

| Job Title | Company | Date Applied | Contact Name | Follow-Up Date | Interview? | Notes |
|---|---|---|---|---|---|---|
| Marketing Analyst | ABC Corp | Feb 15 | John Doe | Feb 22 | Yes | Sent LinkedIn message |
|  |  |  |  |  |  |  |
|  |  |  |  |  |  |  |
|  |  |  |  |  |  |  |
|  |  |  |  |  |  |  |
|  |  |  |  |  |  |  |

> **Tip:** Save the job posting/description. There is often a lag time between application and interviews. By the time an interview happens many times the postings are removed from job sites, or company websites. As such, it can help to pull up the full job posting in terms of what is required and what the duties are prior to an interview. Know the job you are interviewing for and the expectations. Having them top of mind can be really helpful. In addition, if the job is reposted, you know to adapt and change your application as it didn't get called up the first time. Track which resumes goes with which posting/application.

### Assessment: Job Application Success Metrics

- Are you applying to at least 10-15 targeted jobs per week?
- Are at least 20-30% of applications leading to interviews?
- If not, are you adjusting your resume, networking efforts, and follow-up strategy?

> **Tip:** If your response rate is low, focus more on referrals and networking rather than cold applications.

# Mastering Interviews and Storytelling

*"Confidence comes from preparation. Prepare well, and success will follow."* - Unknown

A great resume gets you an interview, but *storytelling and confidence* lands you a job.

## Key Interview Strategies

- Research the company and understand its culture.
- Prepare strong stories using the STAR Method (Situation, Task, Action, Result).
- Practice common behavioral, situational and technical questions.
- Prepare questions that you want to ask at the end of the interview
- Follow up with a thank-you email after the interview.

## Exercise: STAR Method for Behavioral Questions

1. **Situation**: What was the challenge or problem?
2. **Task**: What needed to be done?
3. **Action**: What steps did you take?
4. **Result**: What was the outcome?

Example:

*"Tell me about a time when you solved a difficult problem."*

**Situation:** Our sales team was missing quarterly targets.
**Task:** I needed to identify the cause and implement a solution.
**Action:** I analyzed sales data, identified gaps, and led a training program.
**Result:** The team improved performance by 30% within two quarters.

## Assessment: Mock Interview Practice

Have you practiced common interview questions using STAR stories?

A curated list of common interview questions with answers is provided at the end of the book to help you mold well-structured responses.

# Power Tip: Practice Like a Pro — The Two-Chair Interview Method

Want to truly level up your interview readiness? Try this simple yet powerful method I used to prepare—and it worked wonders:

Step-by-Step: The Two-Chair Mock Interview

1. **Set Up the Scene**
   Place two chairs on opposite sides of a table. This simulates the actual physical layout of an interview room.
2. **Become the Interviewer**
   Sit on the first chair. Ask the first common interview question aloud:
   *"Tell me something about yourself."*
3. **Switch Roles, Physically and Mentally**
   Move to the second chair. Take a breath. Respond as if you're the interviewee:
   *"Thank you for inviting me to the interview. Here's a bit about myself..."*
4. **Repeat the Role Play**
   Keep alternating chairs for each question:
   Ask – Move – Answer – Move – Ask – Move – Answer...
   Cover your full interview script: strengths, weaknesses, career goals, accomplishments, and STAR stories.

## Why This Works

### Realistic Simulation
Physically moving between roles helps your brain distinguish between interviewer and interviewee mode—training you to listen, process, and respond clearly.

### Mindset Shift
This technique helps you **adjust your mindset**, not just your words. You become more confident, conversational, and polished.

### Muscle Memory for Performance
By rehearsing the physicality and language of the interview, you build **muscle memory**. On the big day, your responses flow naturally.

### Reduces Nerves

You've already "been in the room" multiple times—so the real interview feels more familiar and manageable.

**Pro Tip:** Record your responses during practice or rehearse in front of a mirror once you feel ready. Watch your body language, tone, and energy. Improvement comes quickly with reflection.

**Why is it Important to Ask Your Interviewers Questions at the End an Interview? When Employers Ask, "Do You Have Any Questions for Us?"**

This part of the interview isn't just a polite ending, it's actually a golden opportunity. When employers open the floor to your questions, they're looking for the following:

- are you genuinely interested
- have you done your research
- have you been paying attention during the interview or taken notes
- are you seriously considering how you'd fit into the team or company.

### How to Prepare and Make the Most of It

Before the interview, think of 3 to 5 meaningful questions you can ask. Focus on things like team dynamics, company culture, what success looks like in the role, or how the team is handling current challenges. Steer clear of questions you could easily Google and avoid yes or no answers.

This is your chance to flip the script a little. You're interviewing *them*, too. The right questions can help you figure out if this is the kind of place where you'll grow and thrive, and they'll also show the interviewer that you're thoughtful, prepared, and seriously considering the opportunity.

A curated list of smart, strategic questions are provided at the end of this workbook.

# Tips for Different Interview Formats

*"Adaptability is not imitation. It means power of resistance and assimilation."* — Mahatma Gandhi

Whether you're meeting online or in person, mastering the format is just as important as mastering your answers. Use this quick-reference guide to prepare like a pro for every interview type.

## Virtual Interviews

| Tip | Why It Matters |
|---|---|
| Test your tech | Avoid last-minute glitches. Check camera, mic, internet, and platform access ahead of time. |
| Choose the right space | Use a clean, quiet, well-lit background. Minimize distractions. |
| Dress professionally | Full attire matters—top to bottom. Confidence starts with preparation. |
| Look into the camera | It simulates eye contact and keeps you connected. |
| Use headphones | Improves sound quality and reduces background noise. |

Reflection Prompt:

What background will you use? How will you test your tech setup?

## In-Person Interviews

| Tip | Why It Matters |
|---|---|
| Arrive 10–15 minutes early | Shows punctuality and respect for the employer's time. |
| Greet with confidence | A firm handshake, a smile, and eye contact set the tone. |
| Bring printed materials | Resume, references, and questions show you're prepared. |
| Observe workplace culture | Read the environment and adapt your tone and style. |

Reflection Prompt:

What will you pack in your interview folder?

## Panel Interviews (Virtual or In-Person)

| Tip | Why It Matters |
|---|---|
| Research the panel | Knowing their roles helps you tailor your answers. |
| Engage the whole group | Begin with the person who asked the question, then include others. |
| Be concise and focused | Keeps all panelists engaged and shows communication strength. |
| Stay composed | Rapid questions from multiple people test your poise and preparation. |

**Reflection Prompt:**

How will you keep track of panelists and their questions?

## Final Prep Checklist

- I've tested my interview setup or planned my commute.
- I've rehearsed using the Two-Chair Method.
- I've prepared tailored questions to ask the interviewer(s).
- I've researched the company and culture.
- I've practiced STAR stories out loud.

**Power Reminder:** Confidence isn't about knowing all the answers—it's about being prepared to handle the unknown with clarity, composure, and authenticity.

# Negotiating Offers and Making Career Decisions

*"You don't get what you deserve, you get what you negotiate."* - Chester L. Karrass

You got the offer…now what? Many job seekers accept the first offer without negotiating, potentially leaving thousands of dollars or additional benefits on the table.

## Key Negotiation Strategies

- Never accept an offer immediately; express enthusiasm, then ask for time.
- Research salary benchmarks using Glassdoor, Payscale, or industry reports.
- Negotiate beyond salary (e.g., bonus, vacation, remote work, professional development).
- Use data to justify your ask (e.g., "Based on market rates and my experience level, I was expecting $X").

## Exercise: Salary and Benefits Negotiation Role-Play

1. Research the salary range for your role.
2. Write a negotiation script with confidence.
3. Practice with a mentor or coach.

*"Everything is negotiable. Whether or not the negotiation is easy is another thing."* - Carrie Fisher

## Example Negotiation Script

"Thank you for the offer! I'm very excited about the opportunity. Based on my research and experience, I was expecting something in the range of [$X]. Is there room to adjust the salary to better reflect my skills and the market?"

## Assessment: The Decision-Making Matrix

| Factor | Offer 1 | Offer 2 | Offer 3 |
|---|---|---|---|
| Base Salary | | | |
| Bonuses/Stock Options | | | |
| Work-Life Balance | | | |
| Career Growth | | | |

- Have you evaluated the total compensation package, not just salary?
- Does the role align with your long-term career goals?
- If negotiating, have you prepared data and a confident script?

> **Tip:** Always negotiate. Employers expect it, and you could gain 5-10% more with a well-prepared ask.

# Case Study: Mastering Interviews and Negotiation

**Situation:** Zoe, a recent graduate, was nervous about interviews and struggling with salary negotiations.

**Approach:** She practiced using the STAR method and researched salary trends. When she received an offer, she confidently negotiated and secured a higher salary.

**Outcome:** She got a job in her field with a compensation package she was happy with.

Key Takeaways from This Section

- Track your efforts to ensure job search success (3000-Point Rule).
- Organize and track applications for better follow-ups and insights.
- Master storytelling techniques to stand out in interviews.
- Practicing with the Two-Chair Interview Method builds confidence—switching seats between interviewer and interviewee helps sharpen responses, mindset, and delivery.
- Negotiate your salary and benefits confidently.

What's Next?

**The Final Step:** Celebrate your new job and set yourself up for success in your new role.

# Part V - Success – Staying Resilient and Sustaining Career Growth

*"Your work is going to fill a large part of your life, and the only way to be truly satisfied is to do what you believe is great work."* – Steve Jobs

Your job search doesn't end when you land a job. True success comes from maintaining resilience, staying motivated, and continuously growing in your career. This section helps you manage stress, navigate career transitions smoothly, and set yourself up for long-term professional success.

By the end of this section, you will:

- Develop strategies to stay motivated and resilient during your job search.
- Learn how to manage stress and rejection effectively.
- Create a 90-day success plan to excel in your new role.
- Cultivate a habit to express your gratitude to those who enabled your success
- Set goals for long-term career growth and professional development.

# Managing Job Search Stress and Staying Motivated

*"Tough times don't last, but tough people do." - Robert H. Schuller*

Job searching can be mentally and emotionally draining, especially when facing rejections or long wait times for responses. Managing stress and staying motivated is key to maintaining momentum throughout the process.

## Common Job Search Challenges and How to Overcome Them

**Rejection Fatigue:** Reframe rejection as redirection to the right opportunity. Ask for feedback whenever possible.

**Lack of Responses:** Prioritize networking and follow-ups rather than relying solely on online applications.

**Self-Doubt:** Keep a success journal to track progress and positive feedback.

**Burnout:** Take breaks, set boundaries, and create a structured daily routine.

## Resilience Strategies for Job Seekers

- **Adopt a Growth Mindset:** View challenges as opportunities to improve.
- **Create a Support System:** Connect with mentors, career coaches, or peer groups.
- **Visualize Success:** Use affirmations and visualization techniques to stay positive.
- **Celebrate Small Wins:** Every networking meeting, follow-up, or application is progress.

*"The comeback is always stronger than the setback." - Unknown*

## Exercise: Resilience and Mindset Strategies

Reflect on past challenges that you have overcome and how you handled them.

Write down:

- A time you faced rejection or failure.
- How you overcame it and what you learned.
- How you can apply those lessons to your job search.

## Assessment: Personal Job Search Motivation Plan

- Have you established daily habits that keep you motivated (e.g., morning routine, exercise, journaling)?
- Are you setting weekly goals to track progress and stay accountable?
- Do you have go-to stress-relief activities to prevent burnout?

> **Tip:** Remember, job searching is a numbers game; the more consistent and strategic your efforts, the better your results.

# Thriving in Your New Role

*"Success is not just about getting a job, but excelling at it." - Unknown*

Getting the job is only the beginning, how you perform in your first 90 days sets the foundation for your long-term success. Allow yourself the grace of understanding the first 90 days is a period of learning. It is normal and even expected to be uncomfortable during this time.

81% of new hires report feeling overwhelmed with information during the onboarding process (https://www.aihr.com/blog/employee-onboarding-statistics/).

Recognize the majority of new hires, will initially feel out of their depth, experience imposter syndrome, and question their move. All of this is not uncommon. It's okay to feel that, just recognize those are normal feeling and not necessarily the reality.

## Key Strategies for Your First 90 Days

- **Understand Expectations:** Clarify goals and success metrics with your manager.
- **Build Relationships:** Connect with colleagues, mentors, and key stakeholders.
- **Demonstrate Initiative:** Seek opportunities to contribute beyond your role.
- **Learn & Adapt:** Be open to feedback and continuously improve.

Testimonial

*"This workbook didn't just help me land a job. It helped me succeed in my first 90 days. I walked in with a plan and quickly proved my value to my employer." - Samantha R., Project Manager*

*The expert in anything was once a beginner." - Helen Hayes*

## Exercise: First 90-Day Success Plan

Break your first three months into clear milestones:

### First 30 Days – Learning and Observation

- Understand company culture, processes, and team dynamics.

- Have introductory meetings with key stakeholders.
- Set clear expectations with your manager.

Days 31-60 – Taking Initiative

- Start contributing ideas and taking ownership of small projects.
- Find a mentor or buddy for guidance.
- Gather feedback and adjust your approach.

Days 61-90 – Delivering Value and Building Influence

- Take on more responsibility and showcase your skills.
- Establish a reputation as a reliable, proactive team member.
- Discuss long-term career goals with your manager.

## Assessment: Career Growth and Development Checklist

- Have you set short-term and long-term career goals?
- Are you actively building relationships with colleagues and leaders?
- Do you have a learning plan to develop new skills in your role?
- Are you preparing for future career advancements (e.g., promotions, leadership roles)?

**Tip:** Your career success is a marathon, not a sprint, continuously invest in learning, networking, and personal development.

*"Work hard in silence, let success make the noise." - Frank Ocean*

## Case Study: Thriving in a New Role

**Situation:** After a long job search, Omar landed his dream role, but he was worried about proving himself in a new company.

**Approach:** Using the workbook's First 90-Day Success Plan, he set learning goals, built relationships with colleagues, and sought feedback proactively.

**Outcome:** His manager was impressed with his initiative, and he was promoted within a year.

## Key Takeaways from This Section

- Job searching requires resilience, self-motivation, and a structured approach.
- Managing stress and rejection is key to staying consistent and focused.
- You should determine what long-term success looks like in the role, in your first 90 days, be proactive!
- Always look ahead, growth, learning, and career development never stop.

# Gratitude: Your Secret Weapon for Career Success

*"Gratitude is not only the greatest of virtues but the parent of all others."* — Cicero

**Gratitude Is More Than Good Manners — It's Career Strategy**

Success in your job search isn't just about having a polished résumé or nailing interviews—it's also about the people who help you along the way. Behind every milestone is someone who referred you, encouraged you, gave feedback, or simply believed in your potential.

Expressing gratitude to those people isn't just a kind gesture—it's a powerful career strategy. Gratitude demonstrates emotional intelligence, strengthens relationships, boosts your professional reputation, and builds resilience. Research from the University of California, Berkeley confirms that individuals who practice gratitude enjoy stronger social support and higher well-being—key advantages during the uncertainties of job searching.

*"What you appreciate, appreciates."* — Lynne Twist

## Why Gratitude Matters in Your Job Search

### It Builds Relationships
Sincere appreciation reinforces your connections and makes others feel seen and valued.

### It Sets You Apart
Most candidates follow up—few do it thoughtfully. Gratitude leaves a memorable impression.

### It Enhances Positivity
Gratitude helps you stay grounded, motivated, and optimistic, even when facing rejections.

### It Attracts Opportunity
Gratitude opens doors. People are more likely to refer or support those who appreciate them.

## Ways to Express Gratitude

### Email
Timely, specific thank-you notes after interviews or meetings go a long way.

### Handwritten Note
A rare, memorable gesture that stands out in the digital age.

### Small Tokens of Appreciation (if appropriate)

- $10 coffee shop or bookstore gift card
- A thoughtfully selected book
- A LinkedIn endorsement or recommendation

### Public Praise
Shouting someone out on LinkedIn shows appreciation and uplifts others in your network too.

## Who Deserves Your Gratitude?

| Supporter | Why They Matter |
|---|---|
| Family & Friends | Emotional anchors during highs and lows |
| Past & Present Colleagues | Endorsements, referrals, references |
| Professors & Mentors | Career guidance and belief in your potential |
| Recruiters & Talent Pros | Job leads, résumé tips, market insights |
| Networking Contacts | Warm introductions and helpful advice |
| Interviewers & Panelists | Time, attention, and valuable feedback |

*"Gratitude turns a job search into a journey of growth." — Unknown*

## Real Voices: The Power of a Simple Thank-You

*"I sent a thank-you note to a hiring manager after an interview. A week later, she said it stood out—and I got the job. Gratitude works."* — Amanda F., Financial Analyst

## How to Make Gratitude Work for You

- **Be Specific**: Mention exactly what you're thankful for and how it helped you.
- **Be Timely**: Aim to send thanks within 24–48 hours.
- **Be Personal**: Avoid generic messages—tailor your note to the individual.
- **Be Consistent**: Make gratitude a habit, not a checkbox.

## Gratitude Reflection & Action Plan

| Name | Support Given | Gratitude Action |
|---|---|---|
| | Reviewed résumé | Handwritten thank-you note |
| | Career advice and reference | LinkedIn recommendation |
| | Mock interview prep | Email + coffee e-gift card |
| | Shared opportunity at XYZ Corp | Personalized thank-you email |
| | Emotional support throughout | Verbal thanks + family dinner |

# Sample Thank-You Emails

**After a Networking Call**

**Subject:** Thank You for Your Time and Insights

Hi [Name],

Thank you for sharing your experience and advice. I especially appreciated your insights on [topic]—they were truly helpful. Looking forward to staying in touch.

Warm regards,

[Your Name]

**After an Interview**

**Subject:** Thank You – [Job Title] Interview

Dear [Interviewer's Name],

Thank you for the opportunity to discuss the [Job Title] role at [Company]. I valued our conversation and your thoughtful questions. This experience has only strengthened my interest in joining your team.

Sincerely,

[Your Name]

## Self-Assessment: Are You Practicing Gratitude?

Rate each from 1 (Never) to 5 (Always):

| Statement | Score (1–5) |
|---|---|
| I acknowledge people who support me in my job search. | |
| I send thank-you notes after interviews. | |
| I appreciate mentors and peers who guide me. | |
| I publicly recognize others' contributions (e.g., LinkedIn). | |
| I keep track of who I need to thank and how. | |

Interpretation:

- 21–25: **Gratitude Champion** – You're doing great!
- 15–20: **Gratitude Aware** – Keep up the good work.
- Below 15: **Gratitude Opportunity** – Make this a consistent habit.

## Gratitude in Action Checklist

| Action | Done? |
|---|---|
| Sent thank-you note within 24 hours of interview | ☐ |
| Thanked family or friends for emotional support | ☐ |
| Followed up after a networking chat or LinkedIn exchange | ☐ |
| Publicly acknowledged someone on LinkedIn | ☐ |
| Gave a small gift or card for exceptional help | ☐ |

## Case Studies: Gratitude that Created Opportunity

Shoba's Coffee Gratitude

- **Situation**: Shoba, a data analyst, had an informal chat with someone from her dream company.
- **Action**: She followed up with a thank-you email and a $10 coffee e-gift card.
- **Result**: A month later, that contact referred her for a role. She got the job.

Mala's Rebound

- **Situation**: Mala didn't get the job after the final round.
- **Action**: She still thanked each panelist sincerely.
- **Result**: One of them later reached out about an opportunity at a partner firm. She was hired. Gratitude builds bridges—even in disappointment.

# Gratitude Tracker Worksheet

## Purpose:

Gratitude enhances well-being and builds long-lasting relationships. Use this worksheet weekly to stay intentional and consistent.

### Weekly Gratitude Reflection | Week of: _____ |

Name Role/Relationship Support Given Gratitude Expressed? Action Taken/Planned

☐ Yes ☐ No

☐ Yes ☐ No

☐ Yes ☐ No

### Monthly Gratitude Challenge

**Goal**: Thank 5 people meaningfully this month.

Person Method (Email/Note/Gift) Date Thanked Notes/Follow-Up

### Reflection Questions

1. Who had the greatest impact on your job search this month?
2. How did it feel to express your appreciation?
3. Did a thank-you message lead to a new opportunity or reconnection?
4. What's one creative way you could express gratitude next month?

### Final Thought:

Gratitude is more than a feel-good gesture—it's a strategic career advantage. It builds your network, boosts your resilience, and helps you stand out in a competitive job market. But most importantly, it shapes your mindset to one of abundance and connection.

Gratitude doesn't end when you land the job. In fact, that's just the beginning. Carry it with you into every meeting, every challenge, and every career milestone. It's your secret weapon—and it's always in your pocket.

### Key takeaways:

- Set a recurring weekly reminder to reflect and act on gratitude.
- Add your Gratitude Tracker to your career journal or planner.
- Challenge yourself to thank at least one person every week.
- Revisit your self-assessment monthly to track growth.
- Celebrate the impact your gratitude creates—on others, and on you.

# Final Reflection and Next Steps

*"Motivation gets you started, but resilience keeps you going, embrace every challenge as a step toward success."- Sujaykumar Vardhmane*

Congratulations!

You have put in the effort to complete this workbook, reflect on your career goals, and build a solid job search strategy. Now it's time to cement your learnings, set your personal commitments, and move forward with confidence.

This section helps you:

- Summarize key lessons from your job search journey.
- Reflect on personal growth and areas for improvement.
- Create a commitment statement to stay accountable to your career goals.

# Key Takeaways and Lessons Learned

*"The journey doesn't end here; it's only the beginning." - Unknown*

*"Every accomplishment starts with the decision to try." - John F. Kennedy*

*"Go confidently in the direction of your dreams. Live the life you have imagined." - Henry David Thoreau*

Throughout this workbook, you have explored introspection, planning, marketing tools, and action-oriented job search strategies. Now, take a moment to reflect on what you've learned and how you'll apply it moving forward.

## Reflection Questions

- What are the three most valuable lessons you have learned from this process?
- Which job search strategies have been most effective for you?
- How have your career goals or perspectives changed during this journey?
- What challenges did you overcome, and what did you learn from them?
- What habits will you continue to maintain to ensure long-term success?

**Tip:** Reviewing your progress regularly will help you stay on track and adapt as needed.

## Testimonial

*"This workbook helped me take control of my job search instead of just hoping for the best. The structure, exercises, and real-life examples made all the difference." - Lucas G., Finance Specialist*

# Personal Job Search Commitment Statement

*"Failure is not the opposite of success; it's part of success."* – Arianna Huffington

Success in your job search and career depends on commitment, consistency, and a proactive mindset. Writing a personal commitment statement will help reinforce your motivation and ensure you stay focused on achieving your goals.

## Commitment Statement Framework

Complete the following sentence in your own words:

"I am committed to my career success by [specific actions] because [personal motivation]. I will stay resilient, continue to learn, and take consistent action towards my job search and professional growth."

Example:

"I am committed to finding a role that aligns with my skills, values, and aspirations by networking consistently, applying to roles strategically, and preparing thoroughly for interviews. I will stay positive, track my progress, and embrace every challenge as an opportunity to grow."

**Action Step:** Write your commitment statement on a sticky note or in a place where you will see it daily.

_____
_____
_____
_____

## Case Study: Taking Ownership of the Job Search

**Situation:** Nina, an HR professional, had been passively applying to jobs for months without results.

**Approach:** She followed the workbook's Personal Job Search Commitment Statement, outlining specific daily and weekly goals. She also used the Job Application Tracker to measure her efforts.

**Outcome:** Within two months, she landed multiple interviews and secured a leadership position.

# Next Steps: Continuing Your Career Growth

Once you have landed a job, the journey doesn't end, it's just the beginning. Here are some next steps to ensure long-term success:

## Keep Learning and Growing

- Invest in professional development (courses, certifications, conferences).
- Seek mentorship and build relationships with industry professionals.
- Stay updated on trends in your field to remain competitive.

## Maintain and Expand Your Network

- Stay in touch with recruiters, hiring managers, and former colleagues.
- Continue engaging on LinkedIn and sharing insights in your industry.
- Offer help and mentorship to others in their job search journey.

## Set Career Milestones

- Where do you want to be in 6 months? 1 year? 5 years?
- Define clear career goals and take steps to achieve them.
- Have regular career check-ins with yourself and your mentors.

## Key Takeaway

Your job search isn't just about getting a job, it's about building a career that aligns with your values, skills, and aspirations. Stay proactive, keep learning, and never stop growing.

# Appendix

## Tips for Unique Job Seekers

Job Seekers with Career Gaps (Parenthood, Health, Layoffs, etc.)

- **Resume Tip:** Use a functional or hybrid format to emphasize skills over chronology. Mention relevant activities during the gap (e.g., freelance work, volunteer roles, certifications).

- **Interview Tip:** Frame the gap positively: "I took time to [care for family, recover, upskill] and am now fully committed to re-entering the workforce."

- **LinkedIn Tip:** Use the "Career Break" feature to showcase purposeful activities during the gap.

- **Case Study:** *After a five-year career break to raise her children, Sara worried about returning to the workforce. She revamped her resume to highlight her project management skills from volunteering at a non-profit, completed a short certification in digital marketing, and landed a remote role in six weeks.*

- **Testimonial:** *"I thought my career gap would hold me back, but framing my time away as a learning experience helped me regain my confidence. Recruiters responded positively." – Sara S., Marketing Manager*

Moving to a New Industry

- **Resume Tip:** Highlight transferable skills in a "Key Skills" section and showcase industry-relevant projects or coursework.

- **Networking Tip:** Connect with professionals in the target industry via LinkedIn, attend events, and seek informational interviews.

- **Job Search Tip:** Consider an interim role, contract work, or a certification in the new field to gain credibility.

- **Case Study:** *Amit worked in retail management for a decade but wanted to move into tech sales. He emphasized his customer service and sales experience on his resume, took a SaaS sales* certification, and leveraged LinkedIn networking to land his first tech sales role in just three months.

- **Testimonial:** *"I was told changing industries would be hard, but once I tailored my resume and focused on networking, opportunities opened up."* – Amit R., SaaS Sales Executive

Switching to a New Profession (E.g., Marketing to HR, IT to Finance)

- **Resume Tip:** Use a "Career Summary" at the top to explain the transition, linking past experience to the new field.

- **Skills Development:** Gain field-specific certifications or take a bridge role that leverages past expertise while learning the new profession.

- **Branding Tip:** Write LinkedIn posts/articles on industry trends in the new profession to demonstrate commitment and knowledge.

- **Case Study:** *Sandra spent 15 years as a journalist but wanted to move into corporate communications. She highlighted her writing, storytelling, and PR skills in her resume, built a LinkedIn portfolio of corporate-style articles, and secured a communications role at a Fortune 500 company.*

- **Testimonial:** *"I thought I needed another degree, but my transferable skills and storytelling ability helped me pivot successfully."* – Sandra L., Corporate Communications Specialist

Newcomers to a Country (Immigrants, Expats, Refugees)

- **Resume Tip:** If international experience is strong, briefly explain company size and relevance to provide context.

- **Networking Tip:** Join local professional groups, attend community job fairs, and use LinkedIn to connect with professionals in the region.

- **Credential Tip:** Research if certifications or licensing are required (e.g., CPA for accountants, PMP for project managers) and take steps to obtain them.

- **Case Study:** *Jorge, a financial analyst from Brazil, struggled to get interviews in Canada. He attended networking events, secured an informational interview, and enrolled in a bridging program. Within five months, he landed a finance role at a multinational bank.*

- **Testimonial:** *"Networking and getting my foreign credentials recognized made a huge difference. I wish I had started sooner."* – Jorge M., Financial Analyst

**Older, Matured Job Seekers (50s and Beyond)**

- **Resume Tip:** Focus on the last 10–15 years of experience and remove outdated skills (e.g., obsolete software).

- **Branding Tip:** Showcase adaptability by highlighting recent training or certifications in modern tools/tech.

- **Networking Tip:** Leverage industry connections and consider mentoring or advisory roles to demonstrate ongoing value.

- **Case Study:** *Linda, a 58-year-old operations manager, feared age discrimination in her job search. She upskilled in data analytics, refreshed her resume to focus on the last 10 years, and landed a senior consulting role with a flexible work schedule.*

- **Testimonial:** *"I thought I was too old to compete, but focusing on my experience and staying updated with trends helped me stay relevant."* – Linda T., Senior Consultant

**Other Special Scenarios**

- **Career Changers Post-Retirement:** Highlight consulting, freelance, or part-time opportunities aligning with expertise.

- **Former Entrepreneurs Rejoining the Workforce:** Frame business ownership experience as a demonstration of leadership, financial management, and resilience.

- **Job Seekers with Disabilities:** Research disability-friendly employers, use accommodation resources, and emphasize skills over limitations.

**Career Changers Post-Retirement:** *Tom, a retired engineer, started consulting for startups and eventually took on a board advisory role.*

**Former Entrepreneurs Rejoining the Workforce:** *Sara, a former bakery owner, leveraged her financial and marketing skills to secure a corporate finance role.*

**Job Seekers with Disabilities:** *Ali, who has a visual impairment, secured a customer success role by targeting inclusive employers and using assistive technology tools.*

## Neurodiverse and Invisible Disability

Whether navigating ADHD, autism, anxiety, chronic illness, or other non-visible disabilities, your strengths and lived experiences bring immense value to the workplace. Here are some tailored strategies to support your job search journey:

- **Resume Tip**: Focus on your strengths and accomplishments. Use clear formatting and bullet points for structure—especially helpful for those with executive function challenges. Consider using a skills-based (functional) resume if your work history is non-linear.
- **Interview Tip**: Prepare with mock interviews and scripting strategies. If needed, request accommodations such as extended time or alternative formats (e.g., written questions in advance). You're legally entitled to this support.
- **Job Search Tip**: Explore companies committed to inclusive hiring practices. Use job boards like [Hire Autism](), [Inclusively](), and [Chronically Capable]() to find aligned employers.
- **Accommodations Tip**: You are not obligated to disclose your condition unless you choose to. If you do, focus on **how you work best** rather than the diagnosis. Example: "I do my best work in structured, quiet environments and with written communication."
- **LinkedIn Tip**: Consider following hashtags like #Neurodiversity, #DisabilityInclusion, or #ActuallyAutistic to connect with supportive professionals and inclusive employers.

Case Study

Riya, a software developer with ADHD and social anxiety, struggled with traditional interviews. She disclosed her preference for asynchronous communication and completed a project-based assessment instead. She now works remotely at a tech firm that celebrates neurodiversity.

Testimonial

*"I used to feel like I had to mask my differences, but when I found a company that valued my focus and problem-solving style, everything changed." — Riya M., Software Developer*

## Commonly Asked Interview Questions:

### General Interview Questions

1. Tell me about yourself.
2. Why do you want to work for this company?
3. What are your strengths and weaknesses?
4. Where do you see yourself in five years?
5. Why should we hire you?
6. Can you describe a time when you faced a challenge at work and how you handled it?
7. What motivates you?
8. How do you handle stress and pressure?
9. What is your greatest professional achievement?
10. Do you have any questions for us?

### Behavioral Interview Questions (STAR Method)

11. Tell me about a time you had to work in a team to achieve a goal.
12. Give an example of a time you dealt with a difficult coworker or client.
13. Describe a situation where you had to quickly adapt to change.
14. Share an example of a time you went above and beyond at work.
15. Tell me about a time you made a mistake, how did you handle it?

### Job-Specific Questions

16. How do you stay updated with industry trends?
17. Can you walk me through a project you worked on that relates to this role?

18. What experience do you have with [specific skill/software]?

19. How would you handle competing priorities in a fast-paced environment?

20. Describe your leadership style (if applying for a leadership role).

**Situational and Problem-Solving Questions**

21. How would you handle a disagreement with your manager?

22. If you were given a tight deadline on a project, how would you ensure success?

23. Imagine a customer is unhappy with your service. How would you resolve the situation?

24. What would you do if you realized you were going to miss a deadline?

25. How would you approach learning a new skill required for this job?

## Sample Answers to Commonly Asked Questions

### 1. Tell me about yourself

**Sample Answer (To Do):**

"I'm a project coordinator with over five years of experience managing cross-functional teams in the tech industry. I thrive in fast-paced environments and have a track record of improving team productivity by streamlining workflows. Outside of work, I'm passionate about continuous learning and recently completed a course in agile project management."

**To Do:**

- Summarize professional background briefly.
- Tailor to the role you're applying for.
- Add a personal touch (e.g., hobbies or interests).

**Not To Do:**

- Don't recite your entire resume.
- Avoid irrelevant personal details.

- Don't start with "Well, I was born in..."

## 2. Why do you want to work for this company?

**Sample Answer (To Do):**

"I admire your company's commitment to sustainability and innovation. Your recent partnership with [X project] really resonated with me. I want to contribute to a mission-driven team where I can leverage my background in marketing to support initiatives that make a difference."

**To Do:**

- Reference specific aspects of the company.
- Connect your values/skills to their mission.

**Not To Do:**

- Don't say "Because I need a job."
- Avoid vague flattery with no research.

## 3. What are your strengths and weaknesses?

**Sample Answer (To Do):**

"My strength is clear communication, I'm able to break down complex tasks and ensure everyone's on the same page. One weakness I've worked on is overcommitting. I've learned to delegate more effectively and prioritize tasks."

**To Do:**

- Choose real traits, not clichés.
- Show self-awareness and growth.

**Not To Do:**

- Don't say "I'm a perfectionist" without context.
- Avoid strengths disguised as weaknesses.

## 4. Where do you see yourself in five years?

**Sample Answer (To Do):**

"In five years, I see myself in a leadership role, ideally continuing to grow within this company. I'd like to deepen my expertise and mentor junior team members."

**To Do:**

- Align with potential career paths in the company.
- Show ambition and loyalty.

**Not To Do:**

- Don't mention starting your own business.
- Avoid sounding unsure or too rigid.

## 5. Why should we hire you?

**Sample Answer (To Do):**

"I bring a unique mix of experience in sales and customer service, backed by a proven ability to exceed targets. I'm adaptable, quick to learn, and eager to contribute to your team's success from day one."

**To Do:**

- Focus on relevant skills and results.
- Match your value to the company's needs.

**Not To Do:**

- Avoid generic answers like "I'm a hard worker."
- Don't undersell yourself.

## 6. Describe a challenge at work and how you handled it.

**Sample Answer (To Do – STAR Method):**

"At my last job, a key team member left mid-project (Situation). This put our timeline at risk (Task). I reorganized responsibilities, took on additional tasks, and communicated openly with stakeholders (Action). We completed the project on time and improved our process for future handovers (Result)."

**To Do:**

- Use STAR (Situation, Task, Action, Result).
- Focus on what you did and learned.

**Not To Do:**

- Don't blame others.
- Avoid vague or incomplete stories.

## 7. What motivates you?

**Sample Answer (To Do):**

"I'm motivated by problem-solving and seeing tangible results. I love taking a challenge, breaking it down, and creating a plan that delivers impact."

**To Do:**

- Be honest but relevant.
- Tie motivation to job duties.

**Not To Do:**

- Don't say "money" or "titles" alone.
- Avoid generic answers like "success."

## 8. How do you handle stress and pressure?

**Sample Answer (To Do):**

"I manage stress by staying organized and breaking tasks into smaller steps. I also communicate early if deadlines are at risk and find that proactive planning reduces most pressure."

**To Do:**

- Give an example.
- Show emotional regulation.

**Not To Do:**

- Don't say "I don't get stressed."
- Avoid saying you shut down or panic.

## 9. What is your greatest professional achievement?

**Sample Answer (To Do):**

"Leading the launch of our new product line ahead of schedule was my proudest moment. It involved coordinating five teams, managing tight deadlines, and resulted in a 20% increase in revenue."

**To Do:**

- Use numbers if possible.
- Highlight leadership or impact.

**Not To Do:**

- Avoid overly personal or unrelated stories.
- Don't exaggerate.

## 10. Do you have any questions for us?

**Sample Answer (To Do):**

"Yes, I'd love to know more about how success is measured in this role and what the team culture is like."

**To Do:**

- Ask thoughtful questions.
- Show interest in the role and company.

**Not To Do:**

- Don't say "No."
- Avoid questions about salary/benefits too early.

# Questions to Ask at the End of Interview

Based on how the interview has proceeded and the information shared by the interviewer, choose 2 to 3 questions from the list of questions given below. This will demonstrate that you are prepared an interested in the job and company. Choose which of these questions are appropriate at various rounds of interviews.

## About the Job

1. Can you describe the day-to-day responsibilities of this role in more detail?
2. What are the key performance indicators (KPIs) for success in this position?
3. What are the opportunities for professional growth and advancement within this role?
4. How does this role contribute to the overall success of the team and the company?
5. What are the biggest challenges facing the team/department currently?

## About the Team

6. Can you tell me more about the team dynamics and work environment?
7. How does the team collaborate and communicate?
8. What are the team's values and priorities?
9. What is the team's approach to problem-solving and decision-making?
10. Do you have regular team meetings or social events?

## About the Company

11. What are the company's values and mission statement?
12. What is the company's culture like?
13. What are the company's plans for growth and innovation?
14. How does the company support employee well-being and work-life balance?
15. What are some of the company's recent successes or achievements?

## Training and Development

16. What opportunities are available for professional development and training within the company?
17. Is there a mentorship program or opportunities for cross-functional learning?
18. How does the company support employee learning and growth?
19. Are there opportunities for continuing education or certifications?

## Leadership Style

20. What is the leadership style within the team and the company as a whole?
21. How does the company encourage and support employee feedback?
22. How are decisions made within the team and the organization?
23. What is the level of autonomy and decision-making authority within this role?

## Expectations over the First 90 Days

24. What are the key priorities and expectations for someone in this role during the first 90 days?
25. What are the most important things I need to accomplish in the first few months?
26. Will there be a formal onboarding program or a dedicated mentor?
27. How will my performance be reviewed and evaluated during the initial period?

## Job Interview Portfolio Bag Checklist

*(Check off each item as you prepare your Portfolio Bag)*

### 1. Documents

☐ Multiple Copies of Your Resume (at least 3-5 copies, printed on quality paper).

☐ Cover Letter (customized for the role, if applicable).

☐ List of References (with their full names, titles, and contact details).

☐ Work Samples or Portfolio (if relevant to the job, such as designs, reports, or projects).

☐ Certificates or Credentials (degrees, certifications, or licenses mentioned in your application).

☐ Job Description (print or save a copy to review before the interview).

### 2. Stationery

☐ Notebook or Notepad (to take notes during the interview).

☐ Pen (carry at least two, in case one doesn't work).

☐ Sticky Notes (optional, for marking documents or quick reminders).

### 3. Personal Items

☐ Photo ID (you may need this for building security).

☐ Business Cards (if you have them, it's a professional touch).

☐ Breath Mints (to ensure fresh breath).

☐ Tissues or Handkerchief (in case of spills or sneezes).

☐ Compact Mirror or Small Comb (to check appearance quickly).

### 4. Tech Essentials

☐ Fully Charged Phone (ensure it's on silent mode before the interview).

☐ Printed Map/Directions (in case your phone loses battery or signal).

☐ Backup Charger or Power Bank (to keep your phone charged).

### 5. Miscellaneous

☐ Portfolio Folder or Organizer (to keep your documents neat and professional-looking).

☐ Copy of Questions (a written list of questions you want to ask the interviewer).

☐ Water Bottle (optional, but helpful to stay hydrated).

☐ Emergency Contact Info (if traveling to an unfamiliar area).

## Key Reminder

☐ I've double-checked that all items are neat, organized, and professional.

☐ My bag is clean, well-maintained, and appropriate for the interview.

☐ I feel prepared and confident walking into the interview!

# Resume Power Verbs by Category

Here's a comprehensive table of powerful action verbs to enhance your resume, organized by skill category:

This table gives you a progression of power verbs from strong to strongest in each category, helping you:

1. Match appropriate verbs to your specific experience
2. Avoid repetition by having multiple options within each category
3. Adjust the intensity of your language based on the impact of your achievements

When using these verbs in your resume:

- Start bullet points with these action verbs to immediately engage readers
- Choose verbs that accurately reflect your level of responsibility
- Match the verb strength to the significance of your accomplishment
- Avoid overusing the same verbs throughout your document

## Leadership & Management

| Strong Verbs | Stronger Verbs | Strongest Verbs |
|---|---|---|
| Led | Orchestrated | Spearheaded |
| Managed | Directed | Pioneered |
| Supervised | Galvanized | Transformed |
| Guided | Mobilized | Revolutionized |
| Headed | Championed | Overhauled |
| Controlled | Steered | Revitalized |
| Oversaw | Cultivated | Reengineered |

## Communication & Collaboration

| Strong Verbs | Stronger Verbs | Strongest Verbs |
| --- | --- | --- |
| Communicated | Articulated | Negotiated |
| Presented | Persuaded | Influenced |
| Wrote | Corresponded | Mediated |
| Spoke | Moderated | Advocated |
| Collaborated | Facilitated | Reconciled |
| Worked | Partnered | Unified |
| Contributed | Consulted | Bridged |

## Achievement & Results

| Strong Verbs | Stronger Verbs | Strongest Verbs |
| --- | --- | --- |
| Achieved | Delivered | Outperformed |
| Completed | Exceeded | Surpassed |
| Increased | Accelerated | Maximized |
| Reduced | Optimized | Transformed |
| Improved | Enhanced | Revolutionized |
| Generated | Boosted | Catapulted |
| Attained | Elevated | Clinched |

## Problem-Solving & Analysis

| Strong Verbs | Stronger Verbs | Strongest Verbs |
| --- | --- | --- |
| Solved | Troubleshot | Deconstructed |
| Analyzed | Diagnosed | Reengineered |
| Identified | Investigated | Unraveled |
| Examined | Assessed | Disentangled |
| Addressed | Resolved | Overhauled |
| Evaluated | Scrutinized | Reimagined |
| Reviewed | Streamlined | Reinvented |

## Project Management

| Strong Verbs | Stronger Verbs | Strongest Verbs |
|---|---|---|
| Managed | Orchestrated | Spearheaded |
| Coordinated | Executed | Quarterbacked |
| Planned | Administered | Architected |
| Organized | Systematized | Masterminded |
| Scheduled | Expedited | Championed |
| Produced | Implemented | Pioneered |
| Tracked | Monitored | Navigated |

## Innovation & Creativity

| Strong Verbs | Stronger Verbs | Strongest Verbs |
|---|---|---|
| Created | Designed | Pioneered |
| Developed | Conceptualized | Revolutionized |
| Built | Formulated | Engineered |
| Launched | Established | Instituted |
| Started | Initiated | Spearheaded |
| Made | Fashioned | Architected |
| Devised | Originated | Reimagined |

## Technical Skills

| Strong Verbs | Stronger Verbs | Strongest Verbs |
|---|---|---|
| Used | Operated | Engineered |
| Applied | Utilized | Programmed |
| Handled | Maintained | Architected |
| Worked | Executed | Overhauled |
| Processed | Implemented | Innovated |
| Managed | Configured | Optimized |
| Built | Installed | Reengineered |

## Teaching & Training

| Strong Verbs | Stronger Verbs | Strongest Verbs |
| --- | --- | --- |
| Taught | Educated | Mentored |
| Trained | Instructed | Cultivated |
| Showed | Demonstrated | Empowered |
| Helped | Facilitated | Inspired |
| Guided | Coached | Transformed |
| Informed | Enlightened | Revolutionized |
| Assisted | Developed | Galvanized |

## Sales & Customer Service

| Strong Verbs | Stronger Verbs | Strongest Verbs |
| --- | --- | --- |
| Sold | Secured | Captured |
| Served | Satisfied | Delighted |
| Helped | Supported | Cultivated |
| Handled | Addressed | Resolved |
| Provided | Delivered | Championed |
| Processed | Expedited | Maximized |
| Assisted | Facilitated | Elevated |

## Financial & Administrative

| Strong Verbs | Stronger Verbs | Strongest Verbs |
| --- | --- | --- |
| Managed | Administered | Orchestrated |
| Calculated | Reconciled | Restructured |
| Budgeted | Allocated | Economized |
| Reported | Documented | Systematized |
| Filed | Organized | Streamlined |
| Recorded | Cataloged | Consolidated |
| Maintained | Coordinated | Optimized |

# Thinking

Walter D Wintle

If you think you are beaten, you are;
If you think you dare not, you don't.
If you'd like to win, but you think you can't,
It is almost a certain – you won't.

If you think you'll lose, you've lost;
For out in this world we find
Success begins with a fellow's will
It's all in the state of mind.

If you think you're outclassed, you are;
You've got to think high to rise.
You've got to be sure of yourself before
You can ever win the prize.

Life's battles don't always go
To the stronger or faster man;
But sooner or later the man who wins
Is the one who thinks he can!

# References

*Sources are organized by workbook part and reflect internationally recognized research and global workforce practices. Where relevant, regional labour market tools are included as illustrative examples that readers may adapt to their local context.*

**Introduction & Job Search Success Framework**

Bandura, A. (1997). *Self-efficacy: The exercise of control.* W. H. Freeman.

Bolles, R. N. (2023). *What color is your parachute?* (52nd ed.). Ten Speed Press.

Dweck, C. S. (2006). *Mindset: The new psychology of success.* Random House.

Ibarra, H. (2003). *Working identity: Unconventional strategies for reinventing your career.* Harvard Business School Press.

Savickas, M. L. (2013). Career construction theory and practice. In S. D. Brown & R. W. Lent (Eds.), *Career development and counseling: Putting theory and research to work* (2nd ed., pp. 147–183). Wiley.

**Part I – Introspection & Self-Discovery**

Clifton, D. O., & Harter, J. K. (2003). Investing in strengths. In K. S. Cameron, J. E. Dutton, & R. E. Quinn (Eds.), *Positive organizational scholarship* (pp. 111–121). Berrett-Koehler.

Holland, J. L. (1997). *Making vocational choices: A theory of vocational personalities and work environments* (3rd ed.). Psychological Assessment Resources.

Peterson, C., & Seligman, M. E. P. (2004). *Character strengths and virtues: A handbook and classification.* Oxford University Press.

Rath, T. (2007). *StrengthsFinder 2.0.* Gallup Press.

Schein, E. H. (2016). *Career anchors: The changing nature of work identities* (4th ed.). Wiley.

**Part II – Plan: Job Search Strategy & Goal Setting**

Granovetter, M. S. (1973). The strength of weak ties. *American Journal of Sociology, 78*(6), 1360–1380. https://doi.org/10.1086/225469

Kanter, R. M. (1994). *Collaborative advantage.* Harvard Business School Press.

Locke, E. A., & Latham, G. P. (2002). Building a practically useful theory of goal setting and task motivation. *American Psychologist, 57*(9), 705–717. https://doi.org/10.1037/0003-066X.57.9.705

Mintzberg, H. (2009). *Managing.* Berrett-Koehler.

World Economic Forum. (2023). *The future of jobs report.* World Economic Forum.

## Part III – Marketing: Resume, LinkedIn & Job Search Materials

Backhaus, K. (2016). Employer branding revisited. *Organization Management Journal, 13*(4), 193–201. https://doi.org/10.1080/15416518.2016.1245128

Career Industry Authority. (2022). *Applicant tracking systems explained.*

LinkedIn Corporation. (2023). *Global talent trends.* LinkedIn Talent Solutions.

Moran, G., & Brightman, B. (2020). *Resumes for dummies* (8th ed.). Wiley.

Zide, J., Elman, B., & Shahani-Denning, C. (2014). LinkedIn and recruitment: How profiles differ across occupations. *Journal of Social Media for Organizations, 1*(1), 1–14.

## Part IV – Action: Applications, Interviews & Negotiation

Campion, M. A., Palmer, D. K., & Campion, J. E. (1997). A review of structure in the selection interview. *Personnel Psychology, 50*(3), 655–702. https://doi.org/10.1111/j.1744-6570.1997.tb00709.x

Fisher, R., Ury, W., & Patton, B. (2011). *Getting to yes: Negotiating agreement without giving in* (3rd ed.). Penguin.

McCarthy, J. M., & Goffin, R. D. (2004). Measuring job interview performance. *Journal of Business and Psychology, 19*(2), 261–280.

Stone, D., Patton, B., & Heen, S. (2010). *Difficult conversations: How to discuss what matters most.* Penguin.

## Part V – Success: Resilience & Sustaining Career Growth

Duckworth, A. (2016). *Grit: The power of passion and perseverance.* Scribner.

Fredrickson, B. L. (2001). The role of positive emotions in positive psychology. *American Psychologist, 56*(3), 218–226. https://doi.org/10.1037/0003-066X.56.3.218

Seligman, M. E. P. (2011). *Flourish: A visionary new understanding of happiness and well-being.* Free Press.

Watkins, P. C. (2014). *Gratitude and the good life: Toward a psychology of appreciation.* Springer.

Wrzesniewski, A., McCauley, C., Rozin, P., & Schwartz, B. (1997). Jobs, careers, and callings. *Journal of Research in Personality, 31*(1), 21–33.

**Appendix: Tools and Labour Market Frameworks**

International Labour Organization. (2012). *International standard classification of occupations (ISCO-08).* International Labour Office.

Government of Canada. (2023). *National Occupational Classification (NOC).* Employment and Social Development Canada. https://noc.esdc.gc.ca

Statistics Canada. (2023). *Skills and employment trends.* https://www.statcan.gc.ca

U.S. Department of Labor, Employment and Training Administration. (2022). *Competency models.* https://www.careeronestop.org

U.S. Department of Labor, Employment and Training Administration. (2023). ONET Resource Center.* https://www.onetcenter.org

www.ingramcontent.com/pod-product-compliance
Lightning Source LLC
Chambersburg PA
CBHW061112070526
44583CB00027B/3269